1

Tamara Anderson

Printed in the United States of America

First Edition, 2016

ISBN 978-09972879-0-5

Tamara Anderson Books
PO Box 1032
O'Fallon, IL 62269

www.TamaraAndersonBooks.net

Book formatted and edited by Tracy Isley in St. Louis, MO. Cover design by Kenya Leonard © 2016. Testimonies by Jeri Prather and Tiffany Taylor. Scripture quotations are from the New King James Version. Copyright © 1982 by Thomas Nelson. Used by permission. All rights reserved.

Dedication

Ina "Granny" Neal

I would like to dedicate this book to my saving grace, my grandmother, Ina M. Neal, and to the legacy of her grandmother, Lucille McAllister. Granny, as everyone calls her, has always been the matriarch of the family. She was the one that we all called on to pray for us in that time of need. We knew that she had a direct line to God and that He would answer her prayers. I remember as a young girl growing up how she would be in the kitchen cooking and just begin to praise God and speak in tongues. We always knew that granny was either praising God for a miracle or breakthrough or interceding on someone's behalf. Granny would tell us stories of her grandmother, Lucille, and how she was the one that instilled in her this great love for the Lord, and that she was the *true* Holy Ghost filled matriarch of the family. Granny let us know that it was because of her grandmother's intercessory prayer for the family, as well as her faithfulness in serving the Lord, that our generations have been blessed.

Lucille's love for the Lord was deep. My great-great grandfather was not a Christian and he would tell her she couldn't go to church. Back then, the women truly obeyed their husbands so she would rock in her chair humming her hymns. All of a sudden he would yell, "Go head and go!" Granny said that she would grab her Bible and shawl and shout all the way to church. This is how she got the nickname "Shouting Lucy" from the neighborhood. Her great love for the Lord was passed down to my grandmother. As kids we would bet to see who would start shouting first, my grandmother or another mother in the church, Mother Loretta Taylor (who has gone on to be with the Lord). Granny's love for the Lord is stronger now than ever before. It is because of her love and commitment that I have that same love and commitment for my savior, Jesus Christ. So I dedicate this book to her, and to her generational blessing that she has bestowed on us. Love you, Granny!!

For unto us was the gospel preached,

as well as unto them:

but the word preached did not profit them,

not being mixed

with faith

in them that heard it

Hebrews 4:2

Table of Contents

Foreword

It is my delight and great honor to submit the Foreword for this great discussion about faith in Jesus Christ. I am delighted for at least two distinct reasons.

The first reason for my pleasure in endorsing this effort is because of the young lady who has written it. I am so pleased because Sister Tamara (or Tammy, as she is commonly known among her spiritual family) is no "closet Christian." She is a woman who is living the life of Christ boldly. Not in a "holier than thou" way, but in a way that says I love Jesus in a real way, as in I am committed to living a life that is holy and pleasing unto God and I don't care who knows it.

The second reason for my joy in endorsing this effort is because it is about faith. I am a great believer that the just shall live by faith. I have been delightfully tasked with the job of encouraging the members of our church with being "Faithfully Focused." In short, that simply means that the believer is to trust God no matter the obstacles. I am continually encouraged with the teaching of Malachi 3:16 and 17 which says, "Then they that feared the LORD spake often one to another: and the LORD hearkened, and heard it, and a book of remembrance was written before him for them that feared the LORD, and that thought upon his name. And they shall be mine, saith the LORD of hosts, in that day when I make up my jewels; and I will spare them, as a man spareth his own son that serveth him." What excites me is that as people read and share what Sister Tamara has written, God himself will take note of it. When they share it with other people, God will write their names in a book of remembrance. But most importantly, when He comes back He will make up jewels with them. He will remember them as a father remembers His faithful son who serves Him. What a blessing! Furthermore, it strengthens the determination not to let anything steal our attention from being on God and His Word.

Because Sister Tammy has tapped into this great truth and has sought to share it with all who would read this book, I believe that her best blessings are yet to come. It is my highest hope that she will know that the God who has called her and is using her will always be there with her no matter the need. Carry on, young lady. You are doing a great work. Don't let anything drag you down or take your attention from the Lord Jesus Christ.

Maranatha,
Bishop Gregory Wells, Sr., D.D.

Introduction

God has been dealing with me about faith for over two years. It began when I was asked to speak to the women of my church, O'Fallon Apostolic Assembly, by our then new women's president, now Associate Pastor for Members, Dr. Tara Jones. I am truly thankful to the Lord for allowing this wonderful anointed woman of God to be a part of my life. She has blessed me in ways she is not even aware of. Because of her, I have seen parts of the U.S. that hadn't before entered my mind to visit, and she has helped me grow as a leader in the church and to grow spiritually in Christ. Sister Jones had incorporated that the first Saturday of each month would be our Women's Fellowship. She desired that every woman of OAA would come and speak to the other women about whatever the Lord had laid upon their heart. My turn was coming around on Saturday, October 5, 2013, so I began to seek the Lord for what He wanted me to speak to the women about.

One day as I was walking like I did every morning, He showed me a big red door. On the other side of the door I could hear people having a good time. It was as if there were a party. But it wasn't really a party going on. He was showing me my version of what I envision peace, joy, and happiness to be. The big red door was locked and I was holding a gold colored key. While listening to the joy, peace, and happiness on the other side of the door, the Lord let me know that the key I was holding was faith. He told me that faith was the key that would unlock that door. All I had to do was use it. I believe that the Lord is telling us that on the other side of the door is your whatever-it-is that you are longing for and desiring. We have the key of faith in our hand and all we have to do is use it to unlock the door to enter into that wonderful place. God said "with faith." That to me meant that with faith I have the key to unlock any door for access to all the things promised by God. His word says, "all things are possible to him that believe" Mark 9:23. I had what I was to speak to the women about: FAITH.

I began to study about faith. I got up in the morning around 5 a.m. and studied for about an hour and a half, then I would go for my morning walk. I would roll over in my mind all the information I was learning and I talked to the Lord about how to put it together. About two weeks into studying, I was at work when the First Lady of the church I was working at came into my office. She was just being friendly and checking on me as I had only been there three months. As she was just chatting, she began to talk to me about her fears. She was very transparent with me and told me several stories about her fears and how she overcame them. Little did I know that Jesus was beginning a work in me. I thought at the time that He was just letting me know that I had to get over my fears as she had done. That was not the whole story.

The following week as I was returning to work from lunch with a co-worker, a wasp flew into my car. To most that may not be a big deal, but to me it was worth throwing my car into park and jumping out. I was deathly afraid of bugs of all sorts. The co-worker with me tried to get the wasp out but she was unable to help. It took a lady that was at the bus stop picking up her child to get the wasp out. About an hour later I was driving to pick up my daughter, Camille, from school when a circadian flew into my car. Just like the first time, I threw my car into park and jumped out. Unlike the first time, there was no one around to help me with that huge bug. I tried calling back to my job to have one of the young ladies come and get it out, but no one answered the phone. I called three times. It took me over 20 minutes to swat a dead circadian out of my car. Yes, the bug was dead. It died on impact when it hit my purse on the front passenger seat. I knew (after calming down), that God was trying to deal with me about my fear. Not just my fear of bugs, but fear in its totality. So in my studying, I found out that for every force and principle God has created, there exists an active counterpoint. Fear is the active counterpoint of faith. That's right - the complete opposite of faith is fear. For me, this was an eye opening truth.

Upon speaking to the women of my church (another fear I had to overcome), Jesus let me know I was to write this book about FAITH. As I was walking one morning, He spoke clearly to me. He let me know that I was a writer and that I had had this gift since I was a child. He took me back to when I wrote a book about a talking deer. He then brought to my remembrance how I had written down all the other lessons I had learned over the years. As I walked a little more, He even gave me the name of the book, the person I was to ask to do the foreword, as well as the person I was to ask to create the graphics for the cover page. Some time went by, but following a Sunday School class about faith, I knew I had to complete this book, do what God told me to do, and be about my Father's business.

Fear looks; faith...

...*jumps*. Faith never fails to obtain its object.

If I leave you as I found you, I am not God's channel. I am not here to entertain you, but to get you to the place where you can laugh at the impossible.

Smith Wigglesworth

With Faith

Chapter 1

In March of 2008, I learned about faith. This lesson wasn't taught by my pastor during Sunday morning worship. This lesson wasn't taught during bible study (not to say that my pastor has never taught on this subject). I learned this lesson of faith from the Lord.

It had been prophesied to me in 2004 that my husband, Paul, and I would have a boy. But in 2008, we had been married almost five years and still not had a child. I had expressed to him even before our marriage that I believed I couldn't have any more children because I did not have a regular monthly cycle. In fact, it was nonexistent. I was told by one doctor that I was not ovulating, so I was not producing an egg. I was told by another that my uterus was tilted and that I shouldn't even have been able to carry my first child to full term. I was told by that doctor that I had a condition call Polycystic Ovary Syndrome (PCOS) and that I would not be able to conceive another child. But I still knew God was able.

After many years of trying to conceive and after visiting several doctors, I began to speak to my current OBGYN about my concerns. At this point my faith began to fail a bit. He ran some tests. As it turned out, I did not have PCOS. I had irregular levels of certain hormones and wasn't ovulating. He tested to see if my fallopian tubes were open; everything was as it should be. His next step would be to put me on fertility medication that would cause me to ovulate. My husband and I discussed it. Holding on to the prophesy, we really wanted to be blessed by God and to not use the medication to conceive. I am not against fertility medication; we just personally wanted to say that God blessed us and that no man could take credit for this blessing. All of this testing took place in January 2008. In February, I had to have some other testing done due to a previous injury. Before they could do the testing I had to take a blood pregnancy test. It was negative. At this point my faith in God was still quite high. I knew that since everything was ok, (but not necessarily working flawlessly) and since there were no major issues, my blessing was still in His hands.

March came and as I was planning my birthday weekend; my husband and I began to discuss having a baby. We both wanted a boy desperately. We started talking about just taking the medicine because, we reasoned, God gave doctors the knowledge and maybe this was what He wanted us to do. It had been prophesied to me in 2004 that we would have a boy. Relative to the prophesy, I knew they didn't always manifest immediately. It could take a week, a month, a year or even a decade before God's word would come to pass. This concept I knew and should have held onto, but I didn't. As we were talking about this, the devil really began to rear his ugly head. What was just a brief thought, a ten second discussion, became a deep and intense conversation with all sorts of ideas and thoughts flying around. While we had not actually decided to take the medication to try and conceive a child. I did, however, begin to lose faith. Not faith that God couldn't do it, because He is God and He can do all things, but that He wouldn't do it for me. I felt like I wasn't worthy of the Lord's blessings.

This conversation took place on Friday, March 14, 2008 around 2 pm. I will remember this day for the rest of my life. I was the troop leader for my daughter's Girl Scout troop and we planned an outing for that night to go see Disney On Ice. While at the Scotttrade Center, I noticed a little spotting and thought that maybe I was beginning my cycle. On Saturday, March 15, my daughter had a soccer game at 10 a.m. in Hesse Park so the family got up early. I noticed that the bleeding was more than just spotting now. As I got my daughter and myself ready, the bleeding became heavier. This was not normal of any cycle I had ever had. By the time we arrived at the park, I was bleeding pretty heavily and had to return home to change again. This was the first game ever that I had missed my daughter playing in. Once the game was over, my concern started to become overwhelming. I called one of my cousins to get her opinion but she was unable to help. I called my grandmother, who told me to go to the emergency room. I dropped my daughter at a friend's house and my husband and I went to the closest ER. Upon arrival, they were packed. I sat there for over three hours and was not seen. When I tried to plea my case, the nurse told me that my issue was not an emergency and not important even though I was changing about every 40 minutes. We left and went to another ER further out because I needed to know what was going on. I was thinking that something had erupted like an ovary or that there might be a tear in my uterus. This was how my mind worked - always going to the worst case scenario.

Upon arrival at the second emergency room, I waited about 15 minutes before triage was calling me. The nurse collected a urine sample and had some labs drawn. I waited 45 minutes then was called to the back. We were in one room waiting to see the doctor but were moved to another room where I was put by myself. They had my husband wait outside. There was too much blood in the urine sample so they had to catheter me. This was the worst thing I ever had to endure up to that point. Alone in this room with this nurse performing this painful procedure, I found out I was having a miscarriage.

When Paul was allowed in the room, I had to tell him the news and I just began to cry. He was my rock during this whole ordeal. He was also my confidante. I knew immediately what had just happened. I had been trusting God for a miracle, I had had the faith the size of a mustard seed, believing whole-heartedly that He was going to bring this baby boy into our lives, but in one split second I had entertained the thoughts the enemy had brought me. And more than just entertained them; I had actually spoken them, deeply and intensely, to my husband. I did not hold on to the prophesy by faith, rebuking immediately any contrary thoughts. This moment of lapsed faith caused the miscarriage; I have not been able to conceive since. While I had not known at the time that Christ had already fulfilled the prophesy and had done what doctors said couldn't be done, the devil did know and he wanted me to miss out on my blessing. Unfortunately, he won that round. And he didn't stop there.

Following this devastating tribulation, I still had to be a mother, a wife, and a professional at work. I still had to deal with the day-to-day cares of this life. My cousin called me to see if I found out what was causing the heavy bleeding. I didn't want to discuss what had happened with anyone so I lied and told her it was nothing, just heavy bleeding from not having had a cycle in a while. Adding additional stress, problems, obstacles, and challenges is what the devil always does when he has you down. My boss had promised me a promotion, but literally upon returning to work after having been off, I found out that it was given to someone else. Not only did I not get the job but I also had to train the new person to do the job. Talk about adding insult to injury! With this loss now turning into bitterness, I didn't want to be bothered. I would come home and just lay on the couch. I didn't want to be intimate with my husband, I didn't want to be around happy people, and I didn't want to engage in anything. The enemy had me hosting a pity party that lasted way too long. He had me in condemnation. I felt guilty for not holding onto my faith, for lying to my cousin, for not being happy, and for being so bitter. I felt guilty for every wrong thing I had ever done in my life.

But God, but God, but God! Jesus would not allow me to stay there. One day He expressed to me, "you have been here long enough. It is time to get up, dust yourself off, learn this lesson, and get to moving! It is time for you to be about your father's business." Hearing the Lord so loudly and having His presence embracing me gave me the strength to get up off the couch and dust myself off. I have always wanted to be used by God and He was now letting me know that my wish was coming true. It was time for me to be about His business.

My grandmother is a praying woman and I know that during this time she was praying for me. From that day to today, I have not lost my faith in God. When my daughter developed a blood clot in her throat following surgery, I called on my prayer warriors and by faith she was healed in a matter of hours. When we were told that my grandmother was not going to make it after having a major heart attack, I called on my prayer warriors and she is still here today. Also, He has let me know that because He loves me so much I now have a beautiful grandson. God has let me know that faith is the key to unlocking the doors in our life.

We cannot get inside or to the other side of those doors without that key. There is no other way.

How can one come to possess great faith?

Now listen, here is the answer to that: First, the blade, then the ear, then the full corn in the ear. Faith must grow by soil, moisture, and exercise.

Smith Wigglesworth

Chapter 2

WHAT IS FAITH?

Faith, according to Merriam-Webster is:

1a: allegiance to duty or a person: loyalty
b (1): fidelity to one's promises
(2): sincerity of intentions

2a (1): belief and trust in and loyalty to God (2): belief in the traditional doctrines of a religion b (1): firm belief in something for which there is no proof (2): complete trust

3: something that is believed especially with strong conviction; *especially*: a system of religious beliefs.[1]

Faith is belief that something is true. Faith is reliance upon something or someone. Faith is being loyal to someone or something. Faith is powerful. Faith is strong. It can have many definitions or synonyms to many different people. But also, faith is an area in everyone's life that can stand to be elevated to the next level.

Faith According to the World

Our whole life is based on faith. We have faith in our everyday lives and don't even realize it. Without faith, banks and credit card companies would not be in existence. You have faith that when you deposit your money into an account at the bank, it will be available for you to spend as needed. You don't even give it a second thought when you know you have $1,000.00 in your account and you are swiping your debit card for a $3.00 transaction. That's faith. Think back and remember how many times you knew you had money in the bank but your debit card was declined. You knew the bank was in error. Also, banks use faith when lending their customers money. They have faith that their customers will pay back the loan they provided them. Yes, a lot of it is based on credit worthiness, but without faith no one would actually qualify for a loan. Banks can see that you have paid back other creditors that have loaned you money, but if they don't truly have faith that you are going to pay *them* back, you won't get the loan. But take a look around your community and see how many houses are foreclosed. Banks operate by putting their faith in people. Banks have faith that people will pay them back the money lent to purchase a house. Unfortunately, people can fail them. Banking is a system where faith is put in people and not in the Lord.

We have faith that when we go to sit down in a chair, it will not move and it will be able to hold our weight. Think back and see how many times you have put your faith in a chair and it failed you. Paper money, too, would never be accepted without faith. We put so much faith in our currency. I would not be mistaken to say that we put more faith in our money than we do in God. Why is that? The reality is that the value of the dollar is down and its value has continually gone down.

To see more clearly how the price of the dollar has changed, it helps to view price changes over a 10-year period. Let's consider the price of a barrel of oil. Since 2002, the price of a barrel of oil has increased four-fold. For example, if the dollar since 2002 had been as good as the Chinese yuan, the price of oil today would be $82.00 and a gallon of regular gas would cost about $3.10. If it had been as good as the Euro, the price of oil today would be $77.00 and regular gas would cost about $2.90. If it had been as good as the Japanese yen, the price of oil today would be $71.00 and regular gas would cost about $2.75. Finally, if it had been as good as the Swiss Franc, the price of oil today would be $63.00 and regular gas would cost about $2.50.

Even these results miss the full decline in the dollar's value because the values of all of these currencies, too, have fallen over the past decade.[2] The dollar's decline over the past 30 years has been far greater than most Americans realize. It has <u>lost almost half its value</u> against other major currencies since 1985 and is down 33% in the past 11 years alone. Indeed, the value of the U.S. dollar is lower today than it was in 2009 when the recession ended.[3]

The use of credit cards would have to be one of our greatest uses of faith. The very word *credit* is from the Latin verb *crédere* which means "to believe." Credit card usage is truly a two-way street of faith. We have faith in a company that has allowed us to use a plastic card and charge items as we want. Yes, they have given us a limit as to how much we can spend (not American Express), but we still have faith that if we have not hit that limit when we swipe the card, the monitor will read "Approved." These same companies have faith that if they allow you to charge your items, then on a specific date of every month, you are going to send them their payment. We operate using this faith on a daily basis.

I can almost guarantee that most people have never examined this next example of faith in this light. You get up in the morning and begin to prepare for your day. You go to work, you work your pre-allotted time, and you go home. You do this for a week or two or maybe even a month. But at some point, you are having faith in your place of employment that they will pay you for what you have worked. That's right; this is another case where our faith is placed in the hands of someone or something that is not the Lord. In speaking to a co-worker one day at work, he told me that at his wife's job there were several people who had gone to cash their paychecks after having worked all week and the checks bounced. They had faith in their employer that the check that was given to them would be a secure source of payment for their hard work for the week. However, they were wrong. Their employer actually had prior knowledge that the checks were no good, but thought that they could manipulate some accounts to cover the paychecks by the time their employees cashed them. They couldn't. I can't imagine this happening to me and I am so grateful to Jesus that I have not had to deal with a situation like this. But it could happen to any one of us. Just imagine having worked and expecting payment for your services and payment never comes. We function in faith every single day.

Also, when we do something so often it just becomes routine. We do it devoid of any thought. For that reason, we go and start our cars without giving a second thought as to if it will start or not. We have such so much faith in getting into the car, turning the ignition (or using the remote car starter) and hearing the car start, that it's second nature to us. Nevertheless, we have put our faith in the wrong entity. We have all been there when the car didn't start because of a dead battery, a broken starter, or a faulty alternator. In my case it was the fuel injection system. I went to the doctor one day and when my husband and I left the cardiologist's office and got into my truck, it wouldn't start. I knew I was low on gas but my plan was to get some after leaving the doctor's office, so I assumed that if I walked over to the gas station and put a little gas into the truck, it would start right up for me. It didn't. I had to wait for over two hours for a tow truck.

Faith According to the Word

Faith used in almost all of the New Testament scriptures comes from the Greek word *pistis* which means "persuasion; credence (belief that something is true); conviction; reliance; constancy (the quality of being dependable); assurance; and fidelity."[4]

> *Now faith is the assurance (the confirmation, the title deed) of the things [we] hope for, being the proof of things [we] do not see and the conviction of their reality [faith perceiving as real fact what is not revealed to the senses].* Hebrews 11:1 AMP

Faith, in the topical index of The New Open Bible by Thomas Nelson, is defined as "the confidence in the testimony of another." You have this persuasion and proof because you have heard the testimonies of so many saints. You have heard the testimony of how the Lord has healed a sister from stage 3 cancer. You have heard the testimony of how God provided a job for a brother right when his unemployment benefits had just run out. You have heard the testimony of how Jesus came through for someone in the eleventh hour. The word lets us know that

> *And they overcame him by the blood of the Lamb, and by the word of their testimony...* Revelation 12:11

Faith can only be received as a gift from God and it's something that can never be established in and of ourselves. No matter how we might try to initiate faith, we cannot. It is given to us by Jesus Christ according to His own purpose and grace. Yes, we can increase our faith but we can't construct our faith. This is for our benefit so that we don't become full of pride.

> *For by grace are ye saved through faith; and that not of yourselves: it is the gift of God: Not of works, lest any man should boast.* Ephesians 2:8-9

The word reveals to us that faith is God's warranty for us which guarantees the fulfillment of His revelations that He has birthed within His receptive believers. God's warranty is not man's warranty. Man's warranty has stipulations and expiration dates. A magnificent sister who attends the church I do told me that right after the warranty expired on her 50-inch flat screen television, it went out. The company didn't replace her TV because the warranty had stipulations and was expired. However, God's warranty is unchanging, unwavering and guaranteed.

> *God is not a man, that he should lie; neither the son of man, that he should repent: hath he said, and shall he not do it? or hath he spoken, and shall he not make it good?* Numbers 23:19

Also, the revelations that our Lord and Savior have deposited within us have made us victorious and overcomers. Once again going back to the word, it lets us know that whatever is born of God has already overcome the world. There a multitude of scriptures that speak of the revelations received by people from our Lord.

For whatsoever is born of God overcometh the world: and this is the victory that overcometh he world, even our faith. 1 John 5:4

Faith is used as a synonym for *belief* or *believe*. However, for the believer, faith is apparently different from human belief, although it does include it. Belief is like the yeast needed in baking a good quality delicious cake. The yeast is what gives the cake its rise and taste. Belief is the main ingredient of faith. To believe gets us to the door; however, faith is the gift on the other side of the door. We must first believe that there is a God in order to begin to have faith in who He is and what He will do in our lives.

But without faith it is impossible to please him: for he that cometh to God must believe that he is, and that he is a rewarder of them that diligently seek him. Hebrews 11:6

The root of *pistis* is *pĕithō* which means "to persuade or be persuaded."[4] It follows that the core-meaning of faith is divine persuasion. Who are we being persuaded by? The answer should be "The Great I Am," our Lord and Savior, Jesus Christ. As a result, faith is His divine persuasion or marvelous influence in our lives. We have to be fully persuaded that He will do what He has promised and we have to know that these promises will come to pass His way. Abraham had God's promise that he *and* Sarah would have a child. Even though they were up in age and she was past child birthing years, *they* were going to conceive a child. When Sarah took it upon herself to give Hagar to Abraham to birth a child, this was not God's way; this was Sarah's way of having a child. We know the story of how that turned out. We need to understand that faith is God's divine persuasion and what He promises to do He will do, and in His own fashion.

He staggered not at the promise of God through unbelief; but was strong in faith, giving glory to God; And being fully persuaded that, what he had promised, he was able also to perform. Romans 4:19-21

Faith is taking the first step
even when you don't see the whole staircase.

Martin Luther King, Jr.

With Faith

Chapter 3

FRUIT OF FAITH

One of our recent Bible study lessons was taught out of the book *Rebuilding Lives Through the Spirit*, by Elder Michael Boyd, Th.D. My Pastor, Bishop Wells, gave us a homework assignment asking us, "what is the difference between the fruit of faith and the gift of faith?" As I began to study and to do the homework lesson, I had to laugh. God was giving me another two chapters for this book. It let me know that I was on track and that I did hear Him correctly.

As I was studying faith as a fruit of the Spirit, I was in Strong's Concordance and I looked up the wrong translation of *fruit*. Instead of looking up the Greek translation (2590), I turned to the Hebrew word for fruit, which is *chânaṭ*, meaning "to spice up, to make spicy or to embalm."⁵ *Chânaṭ* is a verb, a word that is used to expresses an action, an occurrence, or a state of being. I sat there for a minute because I was confused. This isn't what I had been taught or knew to be true. I always thought of the fruit of the Spirit to be like an actual piece of fruit (noun) that needed to be cultivated and grown. Had I really been walking around in a fog about this subject? Oh, on the contrary! The Lord was taking me somewhere with this.

Natural fruit, i.e., apples, oranges, or bananas, has to grow; it must be matured or ripened to a certain point before it can be consumed. It is similar for a Christian.

For I say, through the grace given unto me, to every man that is among you, not to think of himself more highly than he ought to think; but to think soberly, according as God hath dealt to every man the measure of faith. Romans 12:3

This is to say that everyone who is filled with the precious gift of the Holy Ghost will receive a certain amount of faith. This measure of faith that everyone gets is the fruit of faith referred to in Galatians 5:22-23. Here, the Greek word for fruit is *karpŏs*, a noun. A noun is a word that is used to name something, like a person, place, thing, quality, action or idea. *Karpŏs* literally and figuratively means "fruit," like a piece of fruit, or an effect or result.[6] As we grow and mature in our walk with the Lord, we begin to produce (*chânaṭ* - verb) His fruits (*karpŏs* - noun). In other words, we begin to put into action His name.

> *Abide in me, and I in you. As the branch cannot bear fruit of itself, except it abide in the vine; no more can ye, except ye abide in me. John 15:4*

We cannot produce His fruit if we don't abide in Him nor He in us. This is why I believe the Lord led me to the "wrong" translation. When natural fruit (*karpŏs*) is growing, it is an action (*chânaṭ*). When we as the children of God are maturing, it is an action (*chânaṭ*). While the Holy Spirit is infusing us (*chânaṭ* "to spice," etc.) with these characteristics, it is an action. Each of the fruits mentioned in Galatians 5:22-23 (love, joy, peace, longsuffering, gentleness, goodness, faith, meekness) are *karpŏs*, or nouns - the names of qualities and actions. However, in order to possess these fruits, we have to *do* something. In order to use these fruit, we have to *do* something. In order to keep them, we have to *do* something.

He that loveth not knoweth not God; for God is love.
In this was manifested the love of God toward us,
because that God sent his only begotten Son into the
world, that we might live through him. 1 John 4:8-9

The first use of *love* here is a verb, an action word
expressing a doable activity. It can have a direct object,
someone or something that receives the action. God is love
and His love for us was so great that He did something; He
sent His only begotten son, Jesus, to save the world. We are
striving to receive this AGAPE love to show forth to
others.

> *neither be ye sorry; for the joy of the Lord is your*
> *strength.* Nehemiah 8:10(b)

Joy is a noun, the name given to describe the state of
being full of great pleasure or delight. As I was trying to
really understand what the Lord wanted me to see, I saw
this scripture to mean that because we have been privileged
enough to really know who our Savior is, as we work to
increase this knowledge, He causes us to joy. This joy in
turn becomes our strength that keeps us going from day to
day, and from glory to glory.

> *And the peace of God, which passeth all*
> *understanding, shall keep your hearts and minds*
> *through Christ Jesus.* Philippians 4:7

Peace, also a noun, is the name for having a state of
tranquility. It is similar to joy in that we know Jesus has
already overcome all the issues in this life. In knowing this,
He causes us to have a state of peace as we endure our
tests, trials and tribulations. As He infuses us with His

peace and as we express His peace, it will blow the minds of the onlookers. They will wonder how on earth we can have such peace with all the hell that is going on in life.

> **The Lord is not slack concerning his promise, as some men count slackness; but is longsuffering to us-ward, not willing that any should perish, but that all should come to repentance.** *2 Peter 3:9*

Long-suffering in this context is from a Greek word and is a verb. In English we can use it as an adjective to describe a noun, in this case, "The Lord." Long-suffering here tells what the Lord does and describes how He is; it is all we hope to be one day. I have to be honest and say that this fruit, I find, to be the most difficult to acquire. There is no time limit to long-suffering; it is just a continuous state of doing.

> **Now I Paul myself beseech you by the meekness and gentleness of Christ.** *2 Corinthians 10:1(a)*

Meekness and *gentleness* here are nouns, simply the names for the action or quality of being meek or gentle (mild and fair). Gentleness and meekness, when manifested, is an active display of the state or action of being mild and fair. This state and activity is achieved through the action of humbling oneself. In this sense, when meekness and gentleness are produced, they are working like verbs. Both meekness and gentleness are imparted into us by the Holy Spirit.

> **And the LORD passed by before him, and proclaimed, The LORD, The LORD God, merciful**

*and gracious, longsuffering, and abundant in
goodness and truth. Exodus 34:6*

Goodness (goodness, kindness, faithfulness), is also a
noun, but as I declared earlier, when goodness is
manifested, i.e., actively being produced, it is working like
a verb.

Jesus is temperance (self-control). While there are no
scriptures where our Savior declares that He is temperance,
He did greater than just to proclaim that He is temperance;
He had the greatest showing of temperance that will ever be
demonstrated. With all power in His hands, He remained
on the cross for our sins. He died that we may have life, but
not just life, life more abundantly. No man or woman ever
has nor ever will show temperance like our Savior has
shown for us. This He did so we may know without a
shadow of doubt that He is temperance.

Faith (pistis) is no different from any of the other fruits
(*karpŏs*) of the Spirit in Galatians 5:22-23 in that it is a
noun, the name given for the "conviction of the truth of
anything." God has dealt or given everyone a measure of
faith. With this faith, we must continue to mature and grow
(*chânaţ*) it, as well as to convey it back to the Lord. We do
this with our works. The word is very plain about this:

**Even so faith, if it hath not works, is dead, being
alone.** *James 2:17*

**But wilt thou know, O vain man, that faith without
works is dead?** *James 2:20*

**For as the body without the spirit is dead, so faith
without works is dead also.** *James 2:26*

This is precisely like a grape which has to be watered and needs to have sun and nutrients to grow. Without these things, it dries up. Once a grape dries up, it is no longer considered a grape. It becomes something else, a raisin. This principle is the same with our faith. In order for this fruit to remain alive, we must work.

Let's get an understanding of works. Many believe that our works constitute being baptized or taking communion. It is understandable how these ordinances can be considered works but they are not. They are just that, ordinances - authoritative commands or orders given by God. Baptism is not a work for the simple fact that Jesus told Nicodemus that we must be born of water to enter into the kingdom of God.

> *Jesus answered, Verily, verily, I say unto thee, Except a man be born of water and of the Spirit, he cannot enter into the kingdom of God. That which is born of the flesh is flesh; and that which is born of the Spirit is spirit. Marvel not that I said unto thee, Ye must be born again. John 3:5-7*

If Jesus said that it must be done, and if He did it Himself, then we can take it to the bank that we must do it as well. Communion is not a work for the straightforward truth that Jesus said that we do this in remembrance of Him.

> *For I have received of the Lord that which also I delivered unto you, that the Lord Jesus the same night in which he was betrayed took bread. And when he had given thanks, he brake it, and said, Take, eat: this is my body, which is broken for you: this do in remembrance of me. After the same*

manner also he took the cup, when he had supped,
saying, this cup is the new testament in my blood:
this do ye, as oft as ye drink it, in remembrance of
me. For as often as ye eat this bread, and drink this
cup, ye do shew the Lord's death till he come. I
Corinthians 11:23-26

When we take communion, we are representing,
signifying, and proclaiming the obedience of the Lord's
death until He comes again. *Work*, however, is defined as
"an exertion or effort directed to produce or accomplish
something; a productive or an operative activity; or task."
So our works are what allow us to grow our fruit of faith.

There are works that we must do, and these works that
we perform on a daily basis can either lead us to grow our
fruit of faith and faith in the Lord, or lead us away from
Him and ultimately eradicate our fruit of faith.

> *Wherefore, my beloved, as ye have always obeyed,*
> *not as in my presence only, but now much more in*
> *my absence, work (cultivate, carry out to the goal,*
> *and fully complete) out your own salvation with fear*
> *and trembling. For it is God which worketh in you*
> *both to will and to do of his good pleasure. Do all*
> *things without murmurings and disputing; That ye*
> *may be blameless and harmless, the sons of God,*
> *without rebuke, in the midst of a crooked and*
> *perverse nation, among whom ye shine as lights in*
> *the world; Holding forth the word of life, that I may*
> *rejoice in the day of Christ, that I have not run in*
> *vain, neither labored in vain. Philippians 2:12-16, AMP*

There are many scriptures that speak to works that we
should perform. Jesus started it off in Matthew, chapter 5

during His sermon on the mount. He speaks about works that can grow you in the Lord: almsgiving, prayer, fasting, and most importantly, love. He also addresses those works that can lead us away from the Lord: murder, adultery, retaliation, and judging.

The Bible is very clear that as we are working, we forget not the weak.

> *I have shewed you all things, how that so labouring ye ought to support the weak, and to remember the words of the Lord Jesus, how he said, It is more blessed to give than to receive. Acts 20:35*

We are to give back to those who are less fortunate than we are. We are to be a blessing to others.

John 6:27 explains that we are to work not for meat that will perish but for the meat that will endure unto eternal life. The meat that will perish is worldly gain, but the meat that endures unto eternal life is Jesus. In the following verse, the people wanted to know what work they must do to do the works of God. Jesus replied that they must believe on Him (Jesus) who He (God) has sent. Some may want to stop and say, "oh, all I have to do is believe," but believing (see chapter 5) is just step one. The people in John 6 were following Jesus only to be healed or to be delivered, but they were not following Him because they wanted to be redeemed. Jesus is saying that they had to believe He was sent by God and that they had to want everlasting life with Him in heaven.

> *Therefore, my beloved brethren, be ye stedfast, unmoveable, always abounding in the work of the Lord, forasmuch as ye know that your labour is not in vain in the Lord. 1 Corinthians 15:58*

So, what is the work of the Lord that will grow our fruit of faith? The answer takes us back to

And he said unto them, Go ye into all the world, and preach the gospel to every creature. Mark 16:15

Our work, our job, being about our Father's business, is that of preaching the gospel of Jesus Christ. We are to be out there evangelizing to God's people. We are to spread the "good news" that there is a God who is alive and who cares about His people, that Jesus is soon to return, and that we wouldn't want to miss out on our home going. Jesus directs us that if we believe on Him, we would do greater works than He did.

Verily, verily, I say unto you, He that believeth on me, the works that I do shall he do also; and greater works than these shall he do; because I go unto my Father. John 14:12

These works are healing the sick, raising the dead, restoring sight and hearing, making the lame to walk, and casting out demons. He also said that if we have faith as a grain of mustard seed, not only could we do these wondrous works, but we could also move a mountain.

And Jesus said unto them, Because of your unbelief: for verily I say unto you, If ye have faith as a grain of mustard seed, ye shall say unto this mountain, Remove hence to yonder place; and it shall remove; and nothing shall be impossible unto you. Matthew 17:20

These are the works that will grow us in the Lord and grow our fruit of faith as long as we keep the right spirit.

But please understand that by works alone we are not saved according to the word.

> *For by grace are ye saved through faith;*
> *Ephesians 2:8 (a)*

> *Not of works, lest any man should boast. Ephesians 2:9*

> *And if by grace, then is it no more of works:*
> *otherwise grace is no more grace. But if it be of*
> *works, then it is no more grace: otherwise work is*
> *no more work. Romans 11:6*

As a truth, we are to be about the business of our Savior through our works. We must also recognize that our works are just one part of our salvation walk and they can either lead us to heaven or to hell.

> *For we are his workmanship, created in Christ Jesus*
> *unto good works, which God hath before ordained*
> *that we should walk in them. Ephesians 2:10*

> *Who will render to every man according to his deeds:*
> *Romans 2:6*

> *For the work of a man shall he render unto him, and*
> *cause every man to find according to his ways.*
> *Job 34:11*

> *For we must all appear before the judgment seat of*
> *Christ; that every one may receive the things done in*

his body, according to that he hath done, whether it be good or bad. 2 Corinthians 5:10

For the wages of sin is death; but the gift of God is eternal life through Jesus Christ our Lord. Romans 6:23

In order for us to produce the fruits that we find in our Savior, we have to be filled with the Holy Ghost and to begin to grow and mature. The fruit will be produced as we study the Bible to know the characteristics of Jesus and what He requires of us, as we go through trials and tribulations designed for us because of the need to have some things worked into us as well as worked out of us, and as we fast and pray to get closer to the Lord. As taught in the eighth chapter of the book that this wonderful homework lesson came from, the author says, "The fruit of the Spirit is meant to be a list of qualities that will manifest themselves in our lives when we consciously decide to live according to God's word and be filled with the Holy Ghost." (pg 83)

Faith,

a gift from God,

is one of the most powerful forces governing our universe;

just as the unseen power of gravity works to pull all things

down, the unseen power of faith works to lifts all things

up.

Gene Griffin

Chapter 4

GIFT OF FAITH

The second part of the homework assignment which became another chapter in this book, was to discover what the gift of faith is. The word tells us that

> *Every good gift and every perfect gift is from above, and cometh down from the Father of lights, with whom is no variableness, neither shadow of turning.* James 1:17

Just as God has given us the gift of salvation through our faith, so it is for grace.

> *For by grace are ye saved through faith; and that not of yourselves: it is the gift of God:* Ephesians 2:8

He also gave us the gift of the Holy Spirit.

> *If ye then, being evil, know how to give good gifts unto your children: how much more shall your heavenly Father give the Holy Spirit to them that ask him?* Luke 11:13

The Greek word for *gift* in the James scripture is *dŏsis* which means "gift."[7] The word gift in the Ephesians scripture comes from the Greek word *dōrŏn* which means "sacrificial present."[8] These gifts are given to everyone that yearns for them. They are not only given to people based on their merit, but to anyone who has repented of their sin and desires them. And what I love about Jesus is that He is a liberal giver.

> *If any of you lack wisdom, let him ask of God, that giveth to all men liberally, and upbraideth not; and it shall be given him.* James 1:5

I had to find out what *upbraideth* meant. It means "ungrudgingly, without reproach or faultfinding." Our God, our Lord, our Savior, loves us enough that if we simply ask for these gifts, He not only gives them to us, but he does it liberally without faultfinding to see if we deserve them or not.

Gifts are given for all sorts of reasons. We give gifts nowadays to show appreciation, to celebrate an occasion, or even just to show good will. Abraham gave Abimelech sheep and oxen to confirm their covenant of peace among themselves and future generations. Abigail gave two hundred loaves, two bottles of wine, five sheep ready dressed, five measures of parched corn, two hundred clusters of raisins, and two hundred cakes of figs to David to appease his anger towards Na'bal. The wise men gave Jesus gold, frankincense, and myrrh as a form of worship for who He was and what He had come to do.

While we all will receive some of the same gifts, but our Savior has given certain people certain specific gifts.

> *Now there are diversities of gifts, but the same Spirit. And there are differences of administrations, but the same Lord. And there are diversities of operations, but it is the same God which worketh all in all. But the manifestation of the Spirit is given to every man to profit withal. For to one is given by the Spirit the word of wisdom; to another the word of knowledge*

by the same Spirit; To another faith by the same Spirit; to another the gifts of healing by the same Spirit; To another the working of miracles; to another prophecy; to another discerning of spirits; to another divers kinds of tongues; to another the interpretation of tongues: 1 Corinthians 12:4-10

Having then gifts differing according to the grace that is given to us, whether prophecy, let us prophesy according to the proportion of faith; Or ministry, let us wait on our ministering: or he that teacheth, on teaching; Or he that exhorteth, on exhortation: he that giveth, let him do it with simplicity; he that ruleth, with diligence; he that sheweth mercy, with cheerfulness. Romans 12:6-8

And God hath set some in the church, first apostles, secondarily prophets, thirdly teachers, after that miracles, then gifts of healings, helps, governments, diversities of tongues. Are all apostles? are all prophets? are all teachers? are all workers of miracles? Have all the gifts of healing? do all speak with tongues? do all interpret? But covet earnestly the best gifts: and yet shew I unto you a more excellent way. 1 Corinthians 12:28-31

These lists of gifts are to be understood as representing spiritual gifts. The word *gifts* in all of these scriptures come from the Greek word *charisma* which means "spiritual endowment."[9] Spiritual gifts are those gifts given by the Holy Spirit, as read in 1 Corinthians 12:8. We receive this spiritual endowment not for our own benefit but for the edifying of the church.

*His intention was the perfecting and the full
equipping of the saints (His consecrated people),
[that they should do] the work of ministering toward
building up Christ's body (the church), [That it
might develop] until we all attain oneness in the
faith and in the comprehension of the [full and
accurate] knowledge of the Son of God, that [we
might arrive] at really mature manhood (the
completeness of personality which is nothing less
than the standard height of Christ's own perfection),
the measure of the stature of the fullness of the
Christ and the completeness found in Him.*
Ephesians 4:12-13 AMP

*So it is with yourselves; since you are so eager and
ambitious to possess spiritual endowments and
manifestations of the [Holy] Spirit, [concentrate on]
striving to excel and to abound [in them] in ways
that will build up the church.* 1 Corinthians 14:12 AMP

There are several important factors to remember
concerning spiritual gifts:

1) Every believer has been given spiritual gifts.

*But the manifestation of the Spirit is given to every
man to profit withal.* 1 Corinthians 12:7

As every man hath received the gift; I Peter 4:10(a)

2) The gifts belong to God and are given for the
believer to use for the glory of God.

If any man speak, let him speak as the oracles of God; if any man minister, let him do it as of the ability which God giveth: that God in all things may be glorified through Jesus Christ, to whom be praise and dominion for ever and ever. Amen. 1 Peter 4:11

3) We are expected to use the gifts that have been given to us.

Neglect not the gift that is in thee, which was given thee by prophecy, with the laying on of the hands of the presbytery. 1 Timothy 4:14

Wherefore I put thee in remembrance that thou stir up the gift of God, which is in thee by the putting on of my hands. 2 Timothy 1:6

4) We must accompany the use of our gifts with the right attitude.

But covet earnestly the best gifts: and yet shew I unto you a more excellent way. Though I speak with the tongues of men and of angels, and have not charity, I am become as sounding brass, or a tinkling cymbal. And though I have the gift of prophecy, and understand all mysteries, and all knowledge; and though I have all faith, so that I could remove mountains and have not charity, I am nothing. An though I bestow all my goods to feed the poor, and though I give my body to be burned, and have not charity, it profiteth me nothing. 1 Corinthians 12:31-13:3

5) We will have to give an account on judgment day for how we used our gifts.

For we must all appear before the judgment seat of Christ; that every one may receive the things done in his body, according to that he hath done, whether it be good or bad. 2 Corinthians 5:10

The gifts spoken of here are not on the same playing field as gifts we may give to one another. These gifts cannot be purchased.

And when Simon saw that through laying on of the apostles' hands the Holy Ghost was given, he offered them money, Saying, Give me also this power, that on whomsoever I lay hands, he may receive the Holy Ghost. But Peter said unto him, Thy money perish with thee, because thou hast thought that the gift of God may be purchased with money. Acts 8:18-20

We usually go to a store to purchase a gift that we want to give to someone. But as Peter let Simon know, God's gifts delivered through the Holy Spirit are not for sale and could not be purchased anyway.

One of the deacons at my church is funny and is always joking and playing around, but when it comes to the word he means business. He has been given the gift of faith. He will let everyone know that he has what he calls "crazy faith." That's faith to really believe the impossible is possible, faith that knows without a shadow of a doubt that Jesus is able to do ALL things. There is nothing too hard for Him. This deacon's faith has been increased exponentially. He has been spiritually endowed with this gift in order to witness to those who are still lacking faith. He has been blessed with this gift in order to help others mature their fruit of faith.

Ultimately, the difference between the fruit of faith and the gift of faith is that one is given to every Christian and it must be matured and cultivated: fruit. The other is a spiritual endowment that is meant to be used to edify the body of Christ and not everyone receives this: gift (*charisma*). However, where they are similar is that both come from our Savior and both are needed in the household of faith.

Faith isn't the ability to believe long and far into the misty future. It's simply taking God at His Word and taking the next step.

Joni Erickson Tada

With Faith

Chapter 5

FAITH IS MORE THAN BELIEVING

Faith is distinct from human belief (confidence) or to believe, but it does include it. I always thought that to have faith and to believe were one in the same. Just as we have synonyms, different words that mean the same thing, like *huge* and *gigantic*, I thought that having faith and believing were synonymous. As I began to really study about faith, the Lord let me know that they are not the same. *Faith* and *belief* are very close in meaning but there is a definite difference. The definition of *believe* according to Merriam-Webster is

1a: to have a firm religious faith **b:** to accept something as true, genuine, or real

2: to have a firm conviction as to the goodness, efficacy, or ability of something

3: to hold an opinion: think.[10]

The Greek word for *believe* in 90% of the New Testament scriptures is *pistĕuō* which means "believe, to have faith (in, upon, or with respect to, a person or thing), i.e. credit; put in trust with, by implication to entrust (especially one's spiritual well-being to Christ) -- believe (-r), commit (to trust), put in trust with."[4] *Pistĕuō* is derived from *pistis*, Greek for *faith*, (see chapter 2). To believe in something is completely different than having faith in it. When we believe something, we take it at face value. Contrarily, if we don't believe what someone is telling us, we don't take it at face value. My nephew is a mini encyclopedia. He is always saying, "Aunt Tammy did you know…" then gives me some piece of information that he has heard or read. Most of the time what he says seems to sound like it could be true so I believe him. But there have been several times when he has told me something that I just can't wrap my head around so I don't believe what he is saying. Even so, I don't automatically put my faith in those things that I believe him about just because they sound good enough to be true. In order for me to have faith in something, I must investigate it and get a better understanding of it.

This is the distinct difference between believing something and having faith.

> *There was a man sent from God, whose name was John. The same came for a witness, to bear witness of the Light, that all men through him might believe.* John 1:6-7

John the Baptist was sent to prepare the people for Jesus Christ. He was sent so that he might preach the baptism of repentance for the remission of sins and get the people ready for our Savior. The people were baptized because they believed what John was saying, but faith kicked in once Jesus actually came on the scene and began to work miracles. People come to church initially because they believe in God, but they receive salvation because they have faith in God and His promises.

My Pastor, Bishop Gregory Wells, Sr., while preaching one day, said that faith is one-part belief and one-part obedience. He was saying that faith needs belief in order to be, but it is more than just belief because you have to add obedience to it. I am a visual person, so when I heard this I saw believing being like yellow and obedience being like blue. I learned in grade school that when you mix two primary colors you get another color, so mixing yellow and blue together make green; when mixing belief and obedience together you get faith.

As I was studying this concept of the difference between faith and belief, I came across a blog that really hit the nail on the head for me. The young lady said, "that both belief and faith are an idea, concept, or claim that we are aware of and trust as being true, reality or factual. The difference is in the depth of my awareness concerning my trust on something, not the actual trust, but the degree of awareness I have at the time I speak of my trust in something. That degree is what makes me chose the one word instead of the other. Thus, the common ground between these two words is 1) awareness and 2) trust."[11] Ultimately you have to believe in order to have faith. To believe is the yeast needed in baking a cake and faith is the finished product, the cake. Believing comes first but faith is needed in order to finish the race. Paul understood this when he wrote

That if thou shalt confess with thy mouth the Lord Jesus, and shalt believe in thine heart that God hath raised him from the dead, thou shalt be saved. Romans 10:9

He is letting us know that we must first believe in our hearts that God raised Jesus His Son from the dead. Then

For by grace are ye saved through faith; and that not of yourselves: it is the gift of God: Ephesians. 2:8

God gives us the gift of salvation because of our faith, not our belief, in Him. We go from believing to having faith and He bestows this wonderful, amazing present to us that is salvation.

As I prayed and asked the Lord to help me really break this down, He showed me a staircase. He said that at the bottom of the staircase is belief. Belief is what draws us to the stairs. As we climb the stairs we get trust, trust in God by reading and hearing the word, by fasting, and by praying. As we continue to climb the steps we then arrive to faith. While climbing the steps, we will go through tests and trials so Christ can bring us out as polished gold. While climbing that staircase, we will have learned the characteristics of Jesus Christ, we will have become intimate with Him and we will know that He can do ALL things except fail. Climbing allows us to go from believing in Him to having total faith in Him. The Lord also brought back to my memory a book that my Bishop taught from in bible class, *Blind Spots: What You Don't See May Be Keeping Your Church From Greatness.* In this book Bill McCartney discussed the four levels of relationship: acquaintance, feeling and growth, confidence and trust, and intimacy. It should be all of our desire to get to that fourth level of relationship with Christ, but this can only be done with faith.

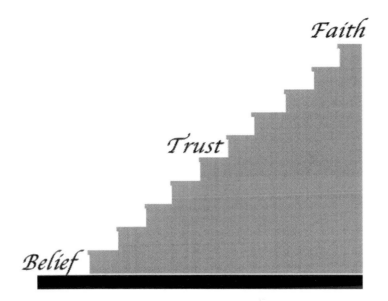

When you find out what the Scripture says about a particular situation, *faith* can be established in your heart; this knowledge will influence your soul (your mind, your will and your emotions).

Unknown

Chapter 6

FAITH THROUGH TESTIMONIES

I own a *Thomas Nelson New Open Bible* (TNNOB) which was given to me by my grandmother. She had used this Bible for God knows how many years. She wrote all over it as she was being given direction from the Lord and as the preacher or teacher was breaking down the scriptures during services. When I began walking with the Lord, she would let me use her bible to study because it is a good study bible. Then one day she told me I could have it. That was over 13 years ago.

In the TNNOB, there is a section in the front called the Topical Index containing definitions of certain words and a breakdown of where you can find the correlating meaning in the scriptures. *Faith* in this section of the bible is defined as "confidence in the testimony of another." *Testimony* is the "witness borne in behalf of something." The meaning of *faith* has already been discussed in Chapter 2 per Merriam Webster and Strong's Concordance. However, *testimony* according to Merriam-Webster is:

1a (1): the tablets inscribed with the Mosaic law
(2): the ark containing the tablets **b:** a
divine decree attested in the Scriptures

2a: firsthand authentication of a fact: evidence
b: an outward sign **c:** a solemn declaration usually
made orally by a witness under oath in response to

interrogation by a lawyer or authorized public official

3a: an open acknowledgment **b:** a public profession of religious experience[1]

The Greek root word for *testimony* is *martus*, which means "martyr, record, and witness."[12] There are three different forms of the word used interchangeably in the New Testament when the word *testimony* is translated; they are *martureō*, *marturia*, and *marturiŏn*. All three of these words share testimony in their description. *Martureō* is defined as "to be a witness, bear record, have obtain a good honest report, testify, give or have testimony, be bear or obtain witness." *Marturia* means "evidence given judicially or generally, record, report, testimony, witness." Last but not least, *marturiŏn* is "something evidential or evidence given, to be testified, testimony, witness."[12] During the editing process, I learned that the stem of these words is Greek *martur-* whose root meaning is "witness, witness of Christ." What a revelation! The Lord was sending me a confirmation that I was his witness.

The scriptures let us know that

> *...faith cometh by hearing and hearing by the word of God. Romans 10:17*

> *So faith comes by hearing [what is told], and what is heard comes by the preaching [of the message that came from the lips] of Christ (the Messiah Himself). Romans 10:17 (AMP)*

Faith comes from us hearing what thus saith the Lord. Usually this scripture is used when someone is referring to the preached word but as I was studying, the Lord let me know that the scripture literally said the "word of God" or as the Amplified says, "the lips of Christ." When we begin to speak about the goodness of Christ, we are testifying. Whether we are at church and stand to give a testimony or if we are out and about with friends and tell of His goodness, someone's faith is being increased.

Faith comes from us hearing what Jesus has done for people, from hearing how He brought someone through a specific situation, how He delivered someone from an addiction, or how He healed someone's body from an illness. We hear about these miracles from others' testimonies. What God has done for them; He will do the same for us. We know this to be true because the word is very clear about this.

> *Then Peter opened his mouth, and said, Of a truth I perceive that God is no respecter of persons:*
> *Acts 10:34*

> *For there is no respect of persons with God.*
> *Romans 2:11*

The scripture also lets us know that

> *And they overcame him by the blood of the Lamb, and by the word of their testimony;*
> *Revelation 12:11*

If faith comes by hearing one another's testimonies and if we overcome the devil by the blood of the lamb and the words of testimonies, then why do we not give our testimonies? When we are blessed it is to be a testimony to someone else. We have to recognize that sometimes when we are blessed, it is not for us; it is for us to be a testimony for someone else. For example, my cousin was completely healed of stage 3 cervical cancer and I can't say that everyone in the family knows. A miracle like this should have been shouted from the roof tops but it wasn't. I only wonder who is getting that same report from the doctor of stage 3 cervical cancer and the news has blown their mind. Just maybe had they heard the testimony of a 23-year-old mother of 2 being totally healed of this same disease, they would have known that this is not the end for them because Jesus has not declared it so. This is why it is imperative for us to tell the good news of how we have been blessed, how we've overcame a particular situation, or of how Jesus Himself came in and intervened on our behalf. If we don't, how can someone else then hear and their faith be increased?

Just as we are blessed for others to know of the goodness of our Savior, some trials we go through are not strictly for us, but are for someone else as well. For over a year and a half I battled with MRSA, a form of staph that is stronger and deadlier. At first I could not understand how I was the only one in the home to suffer with this, but after praying and seeking the Lord on this matter, He let me know that my battle was not due to anything I had done; it was to be a testament for my mother. While encountering the agony and pain of the blisters forming, of having to be cut open and then having the wounds cared for, she was still seeing me give God the glory and continue my work for Him. I was hospitalized twice; the last time, the infection had gotten into my blood and I had to take over two weeks of antibiotics through an IV. But Jesus allowed me to be used to show my mom that no matter what you are going through, He is still on the throne with all power in

His hands, and we have to continue to trust in Him. I now count it all joy to have had the opportunity to have my Job moment.

There is a flip side to the testimonies coin. As I was studying the word testimonies, I noticed that it appeared 23 times in the book of Psalm in the 119th chapter. This observable fact caused me to dig a little deeper. I truly believe that everything happens for a reason and I needed to know what the reasoning was for this occurrence. As I began to read Psalm 119, I was stumped after getting through about the first 48 scriptures. I kept seeing "thy testimonies" over and over again and I was only a quarter of my way through the chapter.

Blessed are they that keep his testimonies, and that seek him with the whole heart. Psalm 119:2

I have rejoiced in the way of thy testimonies, as much as in all riches. Psalm 119:14

Remove from me reproach and contempt; for I have kept thy testimonies. Psalm 119:22

Thy testimonies also are my delight and my counselors. Psalm 119:24

I have stuck unto thy testimonies: O Lord, put me not to shame. Psalm 119:31

Incline my heart unto thy testimonies, and not to covetousness. Psalm 119:36

I will speak of thy testimonies also before kings, and will not be ashamed. Psalm 119:46

The word *testimonies* used in the Old Testament comes from one of two words: *'êdâh* and *'êdûwth* which both have the same definition, "testimony or witness."[13] These scriptures are referring to God's testimonies and for some reason I couldn't quite wrap my head around the true meaning of what was being said. What did the scriptures mean by "thy testimonies"? God does not testify of the good things He has done for someone or how He has healed someone. We hear these testimonies from the person who received the blessing. So what is "thy testimonies"? I began to read the Amplified version of the bible and it did not give me a deeper in depth breakdown like it usually did. I had to go searching.

As I was trying to get a handle on what God was trying to teach me, I went to the internet. I was on a website where I thought I had a pretty good understanding from their breakdown of the scriptures until I read more. We have to be so careful when digesting other people's thoughts and ideologies. As I read further on this particular website where this person was giving a commentary on Psalm 119, they gave an incorrect definition of *precepts*, a word that kept being repeated. As I study the scriptures, I study all of it, not just a section, and this commentary was completely wrong on the meaning of *precepts* from the Psalms. We have to truly seek Christ's face to make sure we are getting His revelation from the scriptures and not our own.

"Thy testimonies" is referring to God's laws or commandments. This is what He bears witness to being wise, good, and just. A commentary by Albert Barnes from *Barnes' Notes* broke it down like this: every rule that a parent gives to their child is a testimony of the parent as to what that parent believes to be good, right and wise.[14] So are the testimonies of our Lord and Savior. However, we as parents sometime don't always give the right testimonies to our children. For example, when my daughter was young, she was the smallest and youngest in her class. She was very social but also timid. By her being an only child, she would allow other kids to push her around in order to have someone to play with. I noticed when she was in first grade that she was coming home with bruises every week. When I questioned her, she would say, "so-and-so kicked me," or "this little boy pushed me." I asked her if she said anything to the teachers and she said she had but they didn't do anything about it. Wanting what's best for my daughter, I instructed her to never ever put her hands on a person first, but if someone did something to her for her to knock them out. Even if she had to use a brick, knock them out. This was not a good testimony to pass on to my daughter because Jesus told us in Matthew 5:39 to turn the other cheek.

But we can take whatever testimonies our God has given to us to the bank. We can stand on them as though they were a solid foundation for the reason that every law of God is His solemn testimony as to what is good and right for man.

The law of the Lord is perfect, converting the soul: the testimony of the Lord is sure, making wise the simple. The statutes of the Lord are right, rejoicing the heart: the commandment of the Lord is pure, enlightening the eyes. The fear of the Lord is clean, enduring for ever: the judgments of the Lord are true and righteous altogether. More to be desired are they than gold, yea, than much fine gold: sweeter also than honey and the honeycomb. Moreover by them is thy servant warned: and in keeping of them there is great reward. Psalm 19:7-11

Good and upright is the Lord: therefore will he teach sinners in the way. The meek will he guide in judgment: and the meek will he teach his way. All the paths of the Lord are mercy and truth unto such as keep his covenant and his testimonies.
Psalm 25:8-10

What are some of God's testimonies that He has given us to obey? We must start with the 10 Commandments, found in Exodus 20:1-17:

- *I am the Lord thy God, thou shalt have no other gods before me*
- *Thou shalt not make unto thee any graven images*
- *Thou shalt not take the name of the Lord thy God in vain*
- *Remember the Sabbath day, keep it holy*
- *Honour thy father and thy mother*
- *Thou shalt not murder*
- *Thou shalt not commit adultery*
- *Thou shalt not steal*
- *Thou shalt not bear false witness against thy neighbor*
- *Thou shalt not covet thy neighbor's house*

Simple version:

- *Trust God only*
- *Worship God only*
- *Use God's name only in way that honor Him*
- *Rest on the Sabbath day and think about God*
- *Respect and obey your parents*

- *Protect and respect human life*
- *Be true to your husband or wife*
- *Do not take what does not belong to you*
- *Do not lie about others*
- *Be satisfied with what God has blessed you with*[15]

The Beatitudes are another set of Jesus' testimonies for us to become wise, just, and good. They are found in Matthew 5:3-12:

- *Blessed are the poor in spirit: for theirs is the kingdom of heaven.*
- *Blessed are they that mourn: for they shall be comforted.*
- *Blessed are the meek: for they shall inherit the earth.*
- *Blessed are they which do hunger and thirst after righteousness: for they shall be filled.*
- *Blessed are the merciful: for they shall obtain mercy.*
- *Blessed are the pure in heart: for they shall see God.*
- *Blessed are the peacemakers: for they shall be called the children of God.*
- *Blessed are they which are persecuted for righteousness' sake: for theirs is the kingdom of heaven.*
- *Blessed are ye, when men shall revile you, and persecute you, and shall say all manner of evil against you falsely, for my sake.*
- *Rejoice, and be exceeding glad: for great is your reward in heaven: for so persecuted they the prophets which were before you.*

If we continue reading in that same book of Matthew, Jesus goes on to talk about similitudes (a comparison between two things), such as murder, adultery, divorce, oaths, retaliation, and love. Please don't stop there; read on through chapter 7. Jesus opens up our understanding of almsgiving, prayer, fasting, wealth, judging, the two ways of life, false and true teachings, and the true way into the kingdom of heaven.

All scripture is given by inspiration of God, and is profitable for doctrine, for reproof, for correction, for instruction in righteousness: 2 Timothy 3:16

While the written Word is our Lord and Savior's testimony and was written several thousand years ago, He has not stop speaking to us, His people. He is daily downloading into our spirits His testimonies. However, He will only lead and direct us in His righteousness and perfect will. It is up to us to have an ear to hear and a desire to be obedient.

Those who don't know my testimony could never

understand my faith!

Antoinette Byers

With Faith

Chapter 7

JERI'S TESTIMONY

One day in 2006, while driving to work I received a call around 6:30 in the morning from my friend, Tammy. She called to tell me to call her grandmother, Mother Ina Neal, who at the time lived in Indianapolis, Indiana. My first question to Tammy was, "Is everything ok?" She told me that granny, as the whole world knows her, was fine and that everything was ok. Mother Ina just wanted me to give her a call. Everyone who knew Mother Ina knew that she was, and still is, a woman of God that stays in God's face interceding for others and has a true gift of prophecy. I used to always joke with her and say that she was Jesus' sister. So being a little scared, I reluctantly ended up calling her on the way into my job.

She told me that God gave her something to tell me. My first instinct was to hope it wasn't bad news because whatever she said that came from God, you could take that to the bank. There were three things that she told me. First, I was supposed to be in ministry as an evangelist. I thought that my ministry was singing. The Lord had gifted me with a beautiful voice and a passion for ushering in the Spirit through songs. I truly thought that I was supposed to minister to people through singing. That's just fear kicking in, because anyone who knows me knows that I hate talking in front of people.

The second prophecy she gave me was that God showed me marrying a Prather. The first thing I said was,

"Prather?!" I was thinking that this was a mistake because Jessie Prather Jr. was already married at the time and his younger brother, Jimmy Prather, was dating someone. Jimmy is my son's godfather, even declaring it before he was born. But I surely wasn't his type and definitely wasn't his age, so I knew it was out the question. She continued to tell me that this Prather plays the drums and God said that was your husband. After that, I was in absolute shock and about to run off the road because she had just described Jimmy Prather. I was truly in disbelief. Nothing like this had ever happened to me. I didn't know how to feel or react.

As I pulled up to my job, she lastly told me that none of this would come to pass until I gave God a complete yes to His will. She said that she would continue to pray and intercede on my behalf because she believes in doing what God tells her to do and say. This would be one of many prophecies yet to come. God will allow things to happen to test your faith and He will put what He says in action. A couple of years passed and I had not really kept the prophecies in the front of my mind, but they were hanging out in the back of it. One day out of the blue I called my mom and girlfriends and told them that on the upcoming weekend I was going to David's Bridal to try on wedding dresses. My mom rode with me; the others met me there. During the ride, I knew my mom thought I was crazy and she even asked me if I had anyone in mind. I told her no, but I knew I was supposed to be married. When I arrived at the department store, we were greeted by the consultant with a list of questions. She asked me the groom's name. My reply was to leave that space blank. She continued with the wedding date. At that time, I said September 17. Keep in mind that this was 2008. The first dress I saw was the only one I tried on. It was just what I wanted; it was perfect and needed only a small alteration. At that time the dress was $1,100.00 and I was absolutely broke, so I prayed over that particular dress and asked God if He would blind the eyes of anyone that was trying to get it. That same year, my time was up at my former church and I decided to visit other churches to hear a word from God.

One Sunday I ended up driving to Alton, IL, to visit Bishop Jesse Prather Sr.'s Church. I have always loved his ministry and preaching style, so I continued to make the long drive every Sunday. I didn't know that God was setting things into motion. By the fall of 2008, I was laid off from my job and my family situation was not so pleasant. My parents had moved in with my son and me earlier that year for what I thought was going to be a short period of time. However, a month or two had turned into six. I decided to relocate my family, Ayinde and me, to Alton. I still hadn't joined the church but since the layoff from my job so many people from the church had opened their homes and arms to me. The love that I felt helped me to finally make up my mind to join. Living Word would be the place that I would wind up getting renewed and restored.

As I slowly come out of my shell in my singing ministry and started allowing God to use me, I began to feel that pull from God. Despite the feeling, I still held back from where He wanted to take me. Years had passed and I was still singing and giving God my all, so I thought. Preachers would come from different churches to deliver God's word and the prophecy told to me in 2006 would always come up. I kept running from God until 2013 when I finally told Him YES from the bottom of my heart. I had gotten so tired of running; it was to the point where my sleep was being interrupted. Throughout the entire time Jimmy and I continued to be friends because he was still a big part of my son's life. Nevertheless, by the beginning of 2014 our feelings started to change for one another. I was still scared of the unknown. The church had been on a 21 day fast and towards the end of it, Jimmy asked me out to dinner. He was very eager to speak with me. When he told me that God said I was to be his wife, I was in shock. It literally took me a few months to believe him.

On Sunday, June 1st, at his birthday celebration at our church, Jimmy asked me to marry him. It was the shock of my life! On Saturday, September 6, 2014, we were married. This is how God worked this out: 2006 was the prophecy and 8 years later (New Beginnings) was the matrimony. The same people that met me at David's Bridal were the same one's in my wedding. The dress that I saw at David's Bridal was the same dress I wore for my wedding. I was able to put it on layaway in 2009; that was the only dress left, not only in the store, but also in the entire region, and it was reduced down to $298.00. Remember, I mentioned that when I registered at David's Bridal originally in 2008, the date I gave them was in September; look at God. But what truly blessed me was not that my focus was on being married, but that it was on doing God's will, and that the woman who God used to give me the word, Mother Ina Neal, was blessed to attend the wedding. The entire wedding was anointed and a blessing for all that attended because we gave God praise in a dance.

One of the points about **distractions**

is that everything they do is destabilizing.

Bruce Sterling

Chapter 8

DANGEROUS D'S

My pastor, Bishop Gregory Wells, Sr., taught a bible class series titled "Those Dangerous D's." In this bible study series, Bishop Wells talked about the five areas where the enemy tries to get us: doubt, discouragement, depression, despair, and distraction. The one area that I want to truly delve into is distraction. As I really began studying about faith and all of the counterparts God was taking me to for this book, the devil came in and used one of those D's my pastor taught on, distraction. When studying the Bible, I use different study aids. One day I was reading a commentary by Albert Barnes from *Barnes' Notes on the Bible,* on Ephesians 6:11. I learned that the devil will not necessarily attack us face-to-face with open warfare, but rather, he will employ cunning, sly and stealthy attacks. As I was writing and studying I began to have a headache every day. I am not a person that will run to the doctor for every little ache and pain. In the beginning, the headaches were tolerable enough for me to function throughout the day, but I would lay in bed in the morning during my normal prayer and study time. Then the headaches became so strong that by the end of my work day all I wanted to do was to go home and lay in bed in the dark. They would even wake me up on Sunday at 4 a.m. and I wouldn't be able to get out of bed until later in the morning. I'm not big on taking medicines, but this drove me to taking pain pills. Still, no matter what I tried, I woke up with a headache every day. I know some people would say to go to the doctor because there must be something wrong, but I didn't have insurance and money was low. Besides, I was trusting the Lord by standing on faith to take the headaches away.

The headaches went on for over a week. I had not touched my Bible, studied the word, nor written one sentence for the book. One morning I was praying to the Lord about it. I had made up in my mind that I was not going to sit around anymore. As I was praying, the Lord let me know that the devil was using my headache to distract me from writing my book. The devil knew how powerful this message was. He didn't attack me face-to-face with a tragedy like losing my job or having a severe car accident. Instead, he came in a subtle way with a headache that would cause me to miss two weeks of church, including bible studies, Friday night services, Sunday school, and Sunday services. The Lord brought back to my memory this teaching of "Those Dangerous D's." I was completely taken aback by this. Christ had revealed unto me one of the devices of the enemy in a real life situation. I told my grandmother the revelation the Lord had given me and she said that she knew it. I asked her why she didn't tell me and she said that I needed to get the revelation for myself. How powerful this was for me. After that, I was more determined than ever to learn about faith. I know that there have been many books written on the subject of faith, but once we get the understanding of just how powerful it is, we have to activate it, to grab hold of it. By faith, there is nothing that we can't do for God, in God, and with God.

Distractions are deployed to destabilize you. The definition of *destabilize* is "to cause something to be unable to continue existing or working in the usual or desired way; to make something unstable."[16] The enemy used headaches to keep me from my early morning devotion time with God. Please know that something that seems small can lead to something bigger. Think of how over time a leaky faucet can lead to an entire house being condemned because of mold.

In this lesson, Bishop Wells brought out peace.

> *Thou wilt keep him in perfect peace, whose mind is stayed on thee: because he trusteth in thee.* Isaiah 26:3

The key to our peace is staying focused on Jesus. The enemy, who was once one of God's chosen angels, knows this and therefore seeks to distract us. One way he sets out to distract us is by using what we see. I was watching the news one night, just wanting to see what the weather was going to be like since we were hitting winter and the stories being discussed reminded me of why I stopped watching the news. Not to say that the news is bad, but out of the dozen or so stories they were reporting, not one of them was upbeat or positive. They were all about negative things going on and not just in my area. There was a story about a child in Florida who might possibly be expelled because of her hair. The Bible lets us know that the eye is the light of the body.

> *The light of the body is the eye: if therefore thine eye be single, thy whole body shall be full of light. But if thine eye be evil, thy whole body shall be full of darkness. If therefore the light that is in thee be darkness, how great is that darkness!* Matthew 6:22-23

Luke has a similar scripture.

The light of the body is the eye: therefore when thine eye is single, thy whole body also is full of light; but when thine eye is evil, thy body also is full of darkness. Take heed therefore that the light which is in thee be not darkness. If thy whole body therefore be full of light, having no part dark, the whole shall be full of light, as when the bright shining of a candle doth give thee light. Luke 11:34-36

Simply put, what you see with your eyes goes to your conscience. Your conscience is a part of the mind that makes you aware of your actions as either being morally wrong or right. If your conscience is full of light (positive/right morals) then your whole body is full of light. But if your conscience is full of darkness (negative/wrong morals) then your whole body is full of darkness. When it declares in Matthew 6:23 "how great is the darkness," please know that a couple of immoral actions can lead you down a slippery slope. I was told of a story about a young man that was a straight A student. He received a full scholarship to a university. Once at college, he began to look at pornography. It was just a little bit here and there but then he became hooked on it. He stopped going to class and his grades started dropping. One day there was a knock at his door and it was the FBI. He had visited a website with child pornography on it and they were able to arrest him on that. He is now labeled as a pedophile and will be for the rest of his life. This is exactly why we need to protect our thought life and actively think disciplined thoughts.

Finally, brethren, whatsoever things are true, whatsoever things are honest, whatsoever things are just, whatsoever things are pure, whatsoever things are lovely, whatsoever things are of good report; if

*there be any virtue, and if there be any praise, think
on these things. Philippians 4:8*

Bishop Wells spoke about three ways we are distracted:
by diversion, by division, and by discord. The enemy uses
distraction by diversion in several different ways. *Diversion*
is "the act or an instance of diverting from a course, activity
or use: deviation."[17] It can also be described as "an attack
that draws the attention from the point of a principle
operation." My pastor brought out selfishness. When we
take our focus off of Jesus and put it onto ourselves, we
began to seek after those things that give us self-
gratification and not those things that are of God. Luke
14:16-21 speaks of how a certain man made a great feast
and had his servant go out to those that had been invited to
let them know it was supper time. Everyone had an excuse
as to why they couldn't attend the feast. They were
wrapped up in things that pertained to themselves.

*For I say unto you, That none of those men which
were bidden shall taste of my supper. Luke 14:24*

In this parable, Jesus is letting us know that if we allow
the enemy to plant that spirit of pleasure-seeking and we
continually are intemperate, then when He returns on that
great day we will not be raptured up with Him. Distraction
by diversion can also be classified with the cares of this life
or deceitfulness of riches. Bishop used the parable of the
soils to break this down for us. In Matthew 13:3-9, Jesus
speaks to the multitude about the sower and the four
grounds that the seed fell upon.

*He also that received seed among the thorns is he
that heareth the word; and the care of this world, and*

the deceitfulness of riches, choke the word, and he becometh unfruitful. Matthew 13:22

This verse lets us know that if we allow the cares of this world or deceitfulness of riches to keep us distracted, we become unfruitful. As discussed in Chapter 3, Gift of Faith, if we are unfruitful then we are no longer abiding in Christ Jesus nor He in us.

Abide in me, and I in you. As the branch cannot bear fruit of itself, except it abide in the vine; no more can ye, except ye abide in me. John 15:4

We do not want to end up like the fig tree that was cursed because it did not bear fruit when Jesus needed it. Lastly, worry, fearful expectations and anxiety fall into the distraction by diversion category. The Lord let me know as I was worrying about a situation that I had no control over, "When you worry, that is saying that you don't trust Me nor have faith in Me." I immediately stopped worrying and completely put all of my trust in Him.

Do not fret or have any anxiety about anything, but in every circumstance and in everything, by prayer and petition (definite requests), with thanksgiving, continue to make your wants known to God. And God's peace [shall be yours, that tranquil state of a soul assured of its salvation through Christ, and so fearing nothing from God and being content with its earthly lot of whatever sort that is, that peace] which transcends all understanding shall garrison and mount guard over your hearts and minds in Christ Jesus. Philippians 4:6-7, AMP

Distraction by divisions comes to us in five types: diverse doctrines, classifications, personalities, racism and sexism. The definition of *division* is "the act or process of dividing something into parts: the state of being physically divided or separated."[18] One of the enemy's core purposes is to cause division among the people of God. The Lord brought back to my remembrance the Tower of Babel. When the people were on one accord, they came together to construct a tower that would allow them to approach God. Their motives were so ultimately wrong. What they were doing was wrong, but on one accord they almost accomplished it, had it not been for God's intervention. What they did was not wrong as far as coming together with one goal in mind is concerned; however, why they were doing what they did was wrong. This instance of harmony and agreement resonated within me. There is power in being on one accord; when we are in unity and on one accord *with the Lord*, we are unstoppable.

Now I beseech you, brethren, by the name of our Lord Jesus Christ, that ye all speak the same thing, and that there be no divisions among you; but that ye be perfectly joined together in the same mind and in the same judgment. 1 Corinthians 1:10

The devil knows that there is power in numbers and unity, so distraction by division of doctrines is one of the weapons he uses against us. In the last days, this distraction by division of doctrines is ever increasing.

Now the Spirit speaketh expressly, that in the latter times some shall depart from the faith, giving heed to seducing spirits, and doctrines of devils; 1 Timothy 4:1

For the time will come when they will not endure
sound doctrine; but after their own lusts shall they
heap to themselves teachers, having itching ears;
2 Timothy 4:3

In August of 2015, I had the pleasure of ministering during an event called *Convoy of Hope*. Over 50 churches in the local Metro East area of Illinois came together with one goal in mind, to help God's people. There were Lutherans, Methodists, Presbyterians, Baptists, Apostolics, people from the Church of God, AME denominational, interdenominational, and nondenominational. On this day we did not let doctrine distract us from assisting over 4,500 people in the local communities. We focused on God and did what He had for us to do - serve His people.

I have been guilty of division by classification (classism) and every time I find myself doing it, I immediately ask Jesus for forgiveness. I have noticed that I don't do it nearly as often as I did before becoming aware of this distraction. Division by classification is the act of treating someone differently based on the way they look or how much money we think they have. We treat those who we believe to be wealthy with more honor and respect, while those we feel are worthless, we treat as such. One Sunday, one of the elders of my church was preaching. In his sermon he was saying that if someone homeless were to walk into the church, we were not to seat him in the back because of how he looked or smelled, but rather, we should bring him to the front so that he might hear the word and desire to be saved. In the midst of him preaching, a homeless gentleman came in. He was seated in the front of the church. Another elder came out of the pulpit to sit with him to show him the love of Christ. During the altar call they prayed over him and I believe they gave him some money. The Bible is very clear when it comes to division by classification.

My brethren, have not the faith of our Lord Jesus Christ, the Lord of glory, with respect of persons. For if there come unto your assembly a man with a gold ring, in goodly apparel, and there come in also a poor man in vile raiment; And ye have respect to him that weareth the gay clothing, and say unto him, Sit thou here in a good place; and say to the poor, Stand thou there, or sit here under my footstool: Are ye not then partial in yourselves, and are become judges of evil thoughts? Hearken, my beloved brethren, Hath not God chosen the poor of this world rich in faith, and heirs of the kingdom which he hath promised to them that love him? But ye have despised the poor. Do not rich men oppress you, and draw you before the judgment seats? Do not they blaspheme that worthy name by the which ye are called? If ye fulfil the royal law according to the scripture, Thou shalt love thy neighbour as thyself, ye do well: But if ye have respect to persons, ye commit sin, and are convinced of the law as transgressors. For whosoever shall keep the whole law, and yet offend in one point, he is guilty of all. James 2:1-10*

Don't let classism distract you, especially from doing what the Lord has called you to do. I have heard too many stories of how someone thought that a particular person was poor because of how they were dressed only to find out later that they were quite wealthy. Don't judge a book by its cover. I am sure we have all heard that saying, and it's true. Angels come in many forms. Whether rich or poor, treat each person as though you were entertaining an angel.

Division by racism is rather self-explanatory. It is simply division based upon our race. It has been said that Sundays at 11a.m. are the most segregated times of the week. Why is that? I am so thankful to Jesus for being planted in the church I am in. My Bishop has crossed this barrier in many ways. He regularly sits down with a group called Conversation in the Community and speaks to them about racism and how to erase this division, particularly in our community and churches. We fellowship with Messianic Jews and churches of different races on a consistent basis. The enemy would love to keep God's children separated in any way, but keep in mind the story of Miriam and Aaron. When they spoke against Moses' wife because she was Ethiopian, God first corrected them then cursed Miriam with leprosy. If Moses had not interceded on her behalf, Miriam would have been a cast away (Numbers 12:1-15). We are not to be divided because of our race or color of our skin. God looks at the heart and so should we.

Division over personalities and by sexism is a simple fix, like division by racism. Yes, we all have different personalities and there are going to be times when those personalities clash. But if we keep in mind the main goal, we can work past this. We need different personalities working together because this allows and breeds different outlooks and ideas. If we only work with people who are like minded, where is the creativity? Don't allow this division sent by the enemy to distract you from doing what you have been called to do and from serving with whom you have been called to serve with. In our church we have leadership meetings called Manna 4 Ministry and in one of them we learned about compromise. When personalities begin to clash, introduce compromise; that way the end goal of "saving souls" is still the key focus. Division by sexism is the same as by racism except it is based on gender. I was quite surprised to find out that there are still some churches that don't allow women in the pulpit. This is not biblical. My intent is not to be disrespectful about this, but just to challenge those churches to seek God's face for a better understanding of that practice.

For ye are all the children of God by faith in Christ Jesus. For as many of you as have been baptized into Christ have put on Christ. There is neither Jew nor Greek, there is neither bond nor free, there is neither male nor female: for ye are all one in Christ Jesus. And if ye be Christ's, then are ye Abraham's seed, and heirs according to the promise. Galatians 3:26-29

Then Peter opened his mouth, and said, Of a truth I perceive that God is no respecter of persons: But in every nation he that feareth him, and worketh righteousness, is accepted with him. Acts 10:34-35

The enemy comes to distract us in so many ways. One of the biggest distraction devises used is the seed of discord. The seed of discord is what grows and causes division in the church, spoken of earlier. Distraction caused by discord is a major offense and the word of God warns us of those who cause offenses.

Then said he unto the disciples, It is impossible but that offences will come: but woe unto him, through whom they come! It were better for him that a millstone were hanged about his neck, and he cast into the sea, than that he should offend one of these little ones. Luke 17:1-2

Discord can be defined as "lack of agreement or harmony between persons over things or ideas: active quarreling or conflict."[19] By sowing seeds of discord, the ultimate goal of the enemy is to divide the body of Christ. This is why it is imperative that we stay unified and when a disagreement comes up, that we settle it in a timely fashion. Discord is hated by God.

> *(v16) These six things doth the Lord hate: yea, seven are an abomination unto him: (v19) A false witness that speaketh lies, and he that soweth discord among brethren. Proverbs 6:16,19*

Discord not only distracts the person who is being entangled in the conflict, but it also is distracting to the person who is sowing the seed. The latter is not aware that they are currently being used by the enemy which means that their focus is not on God. They are not in the place where God needs them to be and they are not being about His business. They are distracted. The former is being distracted and also not in the place where God needs them to be when they are wrapped up in the disagreement. They allow the devil to take their focus off of the Lord and they now focus on this earthly opposition. The word is very clear in Isaiah 26:3 that if we keep our minds stayed on Jesus, He will keep us in perfect peace. Paul was not distracted when some tried to sow discord and annoy him (in this case by preaching the gospel with impure motives and intentions). Instead, *staying focused on Christ*, he rejoiced even the more because Christ was being proclaimed.

> *Some, it is true, [actually] preach Christ [for no better reason than] out of envy and rivalry, but others*

are doing so out of a loyal spirit and goodwill. The latter [preach Christ] out of love, because they recognize and know that I am [providentially] put here [by God on purpose] for the defense of the gospel; But the former preach Christ out of a party spirit, insincerely [out of no pure motive, but thinking to annoy me], supposing they are making my bondage more bitter and my chains more galling. But what does it matter, so long as either way, whether in pretense [for personal ends] or in all honesty [for the furtherance of the Truth], Christ is being proclaimed? And in that I [now] rejoice, yes, and I shall rejoice [hereafter] also. Philippians 1:15-18 AMP

One Sunday while at church, my husband Paul, began to not feel well. He previously had been diagnosed with Antiphospholipid Antibody Syndrome and has blood clots; within one year my husband had four strokes. This particular Sunday in church, he became light-headed and sweaty. We were in the right place for him to receive his healing. I immediately went to an evangelist that I knew would be able to get a prayer through to the throne of grace. I knew she was equipped because she had just the week prior prayed for me while at church as I was having heart palpitations. She discerned them and laid her hands on me and began to pray. They eased up and ultimately stopped as she prayed. So I went to that evangelist to bring that same power in prayer to Paul. Her response was she was unable to pray for him because she had just exchanged words with another sister and was not in the right frame of mind. This evangelist had been distracted by the enemy through discord and as a result was not in her place to pray for someone that was in desperate need. Thank God there were others just as qualified to pray. They did, and my husband didn't suffer another stroke.

The evangelist was distracted by the seed of discord sown by another sister, just as the sister who began the dispute was distracted. We have to be on guard at all times continually keeping our focus on the Lord because the devil is on his job attempting to keep us distracted. She was not focused on Christ nor was she Christ-minded; had she been focused on Him, the comments that led to the argument would not have been made. At that moment she permitted the enemy to use her and for that reason, they both were distracted by discord. We must be careful to not tolerate the devil to use us as the one sowing discord.

> *A naughty person, a wicked man, walketh with a froward mouth. He winketh with his eyes, he speaketh with his feet, he teacheth with his fingers; Frowardness is in his heart, he deviseth mischief continually; he soweth discord. Therefore shall his calamity come suddenly; suddenly shall he be broken without remedy.* Proverbs 6:12-15

In the beginning, distractions are not sin. We all have faced distractions and they are going to continue to come as long as we have breath in our bodies and the devil is on his job. But we are to be *wise as serpents and harmless as doves* as instructed by Jesus when He sent the disciples out to preach the gospel in Matthew 10:16. We have to able to recognize the distractions and have a plan of action to counter them. Distractions becomes sin when we allow selfishness to take control over selflessness. We sin when we allow the cares of THIS life to totally blind us and keep our focus off of the one who gives us life. Sin comes in through distractions that have been sown by the seed of discord then cause any division in the body of Christ. Instead of looking at the negatives being sown, turn it around and find the positive like Paul did in Philippians. We can overcome ALL distractions.

Be sober, be vigilant; because your adversary the devil, as a roaring lion, walketh about, seeking whom he may devour: 1 Peter 5:8

Faith talks in the language of God. Doubt talks in

the language of man.

E.W. Kenyon

Chapter 9

Distractions lead us to doubt God and His many promises begin to seem small or out of reach. Just as there is a progression from belief to faith, there is also a growth from doubt to fear. *Doubt* defined by Merriam Webster is "to be uncertain about something: to believe that something may not be true or is unlikely: to have no confidence in someone or something." In the New Testament, the word *doubt* is translated into 13 different Greek words. Most of them have a very similar definition but for the purposes of getting a deeper understanding of doubt and its guidance to fear, we are going to discuss only two of the Greek translations. The first is *distazō* which means "to waiver in opinion or doubt."[7] The second word is *diakrinō* which means "to separate thoroughly to, from, or by implication oppose, to hesitate, to be partial, or doubt."[20] In studying this subject matter, the Lord showed me that there are two phases to doubt. Phase one is an uncertainty of the mind, a wavering in opinion which comes from the Greek word *distazō*.[7] The story of Jesus bidding Peter to walk on the water to meet Him in the sea is a great description of this.

> *But the ship was now in the midst of the sea, tossed with waves: for the wind was contrary. And in the fourth watch of the night Jesus went unto them, walking on the sea. And when the disciples saw him*

walking on the sea, they were troubled, saying, It is a spirit; and they cried out for fear. But straightway Jesus spake unto them, saying, Be of good cheer; it is I; be not afraid. And Peter answered him and said, Lord, if it be thou, bid me come unto thee on the water. And he said, Come. And when Peter was come down out of the ship, he walked on the water, to go to Jesus. But when he saw the wind boisterous, he was afraid; and beginning to sink, he cried, saying, Lord, save me. And immediately Jesus stretched forth his hand, and caught him, and said unto him, O thou of little faith, wherefore didst thou doubt? Matthew 14:24-31

Peter initially had faith; he told Jesus if it was really you, then allow me to come to you. Jesus obliged him and all He had to say was, "come." This was enough for Peter to jump out of the ship and begin to walk on water. I know that this section of scripture has been used to illustrate many different sermons and bible studies, but Jesus is telling me to use it again. Peter walked out onto the water because he knew who Jesus was. He had just seen him feed over 5,000 people with just five loaves of bread and two fish, so he knew that if Jesus said he could come, then he could walk on the water to come and meet Him. Peter allowed a distraction to come. When it did, he took his eyes off of Jesus and began to look at the storm that they were in the midst of. This distraction then led to doubt. In a split second, Peter went from walking on the sea to sinking into it. It doesn't take much for us to become distracted by the cares of this world. It's payday and we see that our bills out-measure our paycheck. In a split second, the enemy comes and distracts us with a thought like, "how am I going to be able to pay all of my bills?" This distraction can lead us straightway into doubt if we don't nip it in the bud right there. We know that off the bat that we should pay our tithes. No matter what, we have been commanded to give the Lord 1/10 of our wages.

And all the tithe of the land, whether of the seed of the land, or of the fruit of the tree, is the Lord's: it is holy unto the Lord. And if a man will at all redeem ought of his tithes, he shall add thereto the fifth part thereof. And concerning the tithe of the herd, or of the flock, even of whatsoever passeth under the rod, the tenth shall be holy unto the Lord. Leviticus 27:30-32

Honour the Lord with thy substance, and with the firstfruits of all thine increase: Proverbs 3:9

And Jesus answering said unto them, Render to Caesar the things that are Caesar's, and to God the things that are God's. And they marvelled at him. Mark 12:17

Doubt then comes in and begins to rear its ugly head and we say to ourselves, "if I don't pay my tithes this week I might be able to swing this." Phase one of doubt looks just like this. We know what we are supposed to do but we waiver in our mind or are uncertain of what actions to actually take. We become skeptical in our commitment to the choices that we know we should make. There is just a sliver of doubt there. When Jesus says to Peter, "O thou of little faith, wherefore didst thou doubt?" doubt in this scripture is translated from *distazō,* "waiver." Just as we know that we are supposed to pay our tithes without having any doubt and that the Lord will supply all of our needs,

Peter should not have doubted and should have continued to walk to Jesus.

Another great example of phase one of doubt is the story of Thomas. Thomas was one of the original 12 disciples that walked with Jesus throughout His three years of ministry. Thomas was there when Jesus told His disciples that He was going to be crucified but that he would see them again in Galilee after His resurrection (Matthew 26:32, Mark 14:28). So if Thomas heard from out of Jesus' mouth that he would see Him again, there should not have been any doubt when the other ten disciples told Thomas that they had seen Jesus, nor upon Thomas' initially being able to see Jesus for himself.

> *But Thomas, one of the twelve, called Didymus, was not with them when Jesus came. The other disciples therefore said unto him, We have seen the Lord. But he said unto them, Except I shall see in his hands the print of the nails, and put my finger into the print of the nails, and thrust my hand into his side, I will not believe. John 20:24-25*

> *Then the eleven disciples went away into Galilee, into a mountain where Jesus had appointed them. And when they saw him, they worshipped him: but some doubted. Matthew 28:16-17*

Thomas was walking in phase one of doubt. It wasn't until he was able to actually touch the wounds of Christ that he was doubt free.

> *And after eight days again his disciples were within, and Thomas with them: then came Jesus, the doors being shut, and stood in the midst, and said, Peace*

be unto you. Then saith he to Thomas, Reach hither thy finger, and behold my hands; and reach hither thy hand, and thrust it into my side: and be not faithless, but believing. And Thomas answered and said unto him, My Lord and my God. Jesus saith unto him, Thomas, because thou hast seen me, thou hast believed: blessed are they that have not seen, and yet have believed. John 20:26-29

If we don't utterly subdue our doubt in phase one, it will grow and shift us into phase two of doubt. Phase two doubt comes from the Greek word *diakrinō* which means "to separate thoroughly to, from, or by implication oppose, to hesitate, to be partial, or doubt."[20] In phase two of doubt, we have chosen to thoroughly separate ourselves from, or completely oppose something that we once believed to be true. This can occur if we had initially believed Christ for something that may not have manifested in what we perceived to be a timely manner, e.g., healing of a sickness or assumed unanswered prayer. These circumstances tend to cause us to doubt God's goodness. Another reason may be from having been taught a foundational principle, but then someone comes along and begins to teach you that same subject matter but differently, e.g., baptism in Jesus' name vs. in the name of the Father, Son and Holy Ghost. Phase one doubt is manifested in our minds; however, phase two doubt is established in our hearts.

For verily I say unto you, That whosoever shall say unto this mountain, Be thou removed, and be thou cast into the sea; and shall not doubt in his heart, but shall believe that those things which he saith shall

come to pass; he shall have whatsoever he saith.
Mark 11:23

We all will face doubt just as we will face distractions, but it is our responsibility to be on guard to fight against them. Imagine a crack in a sidewalk. If not sealed immediately, a weed can begin to grow there. That crack allows just enough rain and sunshine to get through for a weed to germinate. If it is caught early enough and weed killer is applied, the weed will die and the crack can be closed; however, if it is permitted to grow completely unchecked, the weed will grow and will cause a small crack to turn into a major crack that will ultimately lead to structural damage. This is how doubt can grow. The enemy begins by planting a single thought that is contradictory to what we know to be true. If we don't speak against that thought with the word of God, then it will begin to develop as doubt in our psyche or soul.

All doubt comes from satan himself, whether he does it directly like he did when he tempted Jesus after He had fasted 40 days and nights (Matthew 4:1-11), or whether he uses someone or something like he did in the Garden of Eden when the serpent caused Eve to doubt what God said about eating from the tree of the knowledge of good and evil (Genesis 3:1-7). One way satan brings about doubt is through intellect. The world has its own worldly wisdom; whose viewpoints are in obvious resistance to godly wisdom.

Among them the god of this world [Satan] has blinded the minds of the unbelieving to prevent them from seeing the illuminating light of the gospel of the glory of Christ, who is the image of God.

2 Corinthians 4:4 (AMP)

But the wisdom that is from above is first pure, then peaceable, gentle, and easy to be intreated, full of mercy and good fruits, without partiality, and without hypocrisy. *James 3:17*

For the Lord giveth wisdom: out of his mouth cometh knowledge and understanding. *Proverbs 2:6*

The greatest illustration of this is Darwin's evolution theory. In general, it states that one day there was a big bang and everything evolved from one single celled organism. The word is very clear that in the beginning God created the heaven and the earth as well as light and everything else. Understanding that doubt begins as a thought, what better way to plant it than through worldly education. I am not against education and obtaining higher degrees of learning, but ask yourself this question, "does what I'm learning edify the body of Christ?"

One of the most significant times the devil will attack Christians with doubt is after we have performed a sin. The instant we commit a sin; we begin to doubt our salvation. The enemy knows the word just like we do. Going back to Matthew 4:1-11, when he came at Jesus he spoke to Him using the word. He will do the same to us; after sinning, the devil will come with the word.

Whosoever is born of God doth not commit sin; for his seed remaineth in him: and he cannot sin, because he is born of God. *1 John 3:9*

But we are to do as Jesus did and come back at him with the word.

For all have sinned, and come short of the glory of God; Romans 3:23

However, we are not to continually sin based on this scripture. We are to mature spiritually.

There is a remedy for doubt. First and foremost, we must study the word of God. We can't fight against anything, any thought, or against satan without having the unadulterated word living on the inside. In phase one of doubt, just simply speak to the enemy the truth concerning whatever the thought is that he has planted that is contradictory to what you know to be true. Let's say it's paying tithes; immediately we can speak to that thought and to the devil what the word says.

(v30) And all the tithe of the land, whether of the seed of the land, or of the fruit of the tree, is the Lord's: it is holy unto the Lord. (v32) And concerning the tithe of the herd, or of the flock, even of whatsoever passeth under the rod, the tenth shall be holy unto the Lord. Leviticus 27:30, 32

If we know what the word says about any situation, then the doubt has no room to manifest past phase one. But on the off chance that it does increase and reaches phase two, then confess the doubt to the Lord. He is God and he already knows what we are going through. He will forgive us when we confess our doubts to Him.

If we confess our sins, he is faithful and just to forgive us our sins, and to cleanse us from all unrighteousness. 1 John 1:9

And lastly, earnestly pray. The best way to overcome doubt when we're faced with it is to look back at all the answered prayers of our past. We need to create a vivacious cycle of "the more I pray with faith, the more the Lord will answer my prayers. The more my prayers are answered, the greater my faith will become. The greater my faith, the fewer cracks there are for doubt." This is why it is pertinent that we rein doubt in while it is just a thought, because if we don't, our doubt in the mind will grow into doubt in the heart. Just like distractions can become sin if not dealt with, doubt that is in the heart can lead to unbelief, which is a sin.

Faith is: dead to doubts, dumb to discouragements, blind to impossibilities.

Unknown

Chapter 10

UNBELIEF

In a positive sense, just as John the Baptist paved the way for Jesus Christ by baptizing the people for the remission of sins, in the negative, doubt paves the way for unbelief. When we don't completely eradicate doubt but instead allow it to fester in our hearts, it generates unbelief. When looking up the definition for unbelief, I was rather shocked to see how the world defines it. *Unbelief* is explained as "a lack of religious belief; incredulity or skepticism especially in matters of religious faith."[21] To see that the meaning of this word is aligned with religion had me questioning, does the world then not have unbelief when it comes to other matters? Looking further into this, the world doesn't use *unbelief* when referring to not being able to accept something as true. Generally, we say *disbelief*. The word *disbelief* is not in the bible at all, only *unbelief*. Another thing that caught my attention was that *disbelief* is described as a feeling whereas *unbelief* is a lack of belief. As I was researching this chapter, the Lord was letting me know that unbelief is a serious condition that must be addressed and dealt with properly.

The word *unbelief* is used to depict two types of people in the bible. The first type comes from the Greek word *apistia* (*a-* "not" + *pistós* "faithful") which means "faithlessness, disbelief (but a want of Christian faith), unfaithfulness (disobedience) – unbelief." The second type comes from the Greek word *apĕithĕia* (*a-* "not" + *pĕithō* "persuaded") which means "disbelief (obstinate and rebellious) – disobedience, unbelief."[22]

The first thing that the Lord brought to my attention was that the definition of *unbelief, apistia,* was "a wanting of Christian faith," whereas the definition of *unbelief, apĕithĕia,* was the complete opposite, using the words "obstinate" and "rebellious." The story of the demon possessed son in Mark 9:14-27 exemplifies *unbelief* as a wanting of Christian faith. A father brought his son to the apostles to be healed of the dumb spirit, but the apostles couldn't cast it out. When Jesus came down from the mountain, he told the father that his son would be healed if he only believed. The father believed because he had brought his son there in the first place, but he also understood that this was something new to him and that therefore there might be areas of his heart or mind in which there might still lay some unbelief. So, he earnestly asked Jesus to help his unbelief. This story is a perfect example of the kind of unbelief that although it is still resonating within us, we want it banished and we want that place filled with faith. I believe that we as Christians who have allowed our doubt to develop into unbelief but know that we need help with it, and who are seeking the Lord to help our unbelief, live here. But there are many others who are walking around in that second type of unbelief. While unbelief is a sin, those in that second category are so much more in trouble than the first.

The second type of unbelief is exemplified by the Pharisees and scribes that would come to antagonize Jesus as he taught and healed the people. Their unbelief was obstinate and a form of rebellion. They were not going to change what they believed nor what they were doing, no matter what Jesus said to them. They were without Christian faith, or as we would say, heathens.

He answered and said unto them, Well hath Esaias
prophesied of you hypocrites, as it is written, This
people honoureth me with their lips, but their heart
is far from me. Howbeit in vain do they worship me,
teaching for doctrines the commandments of men.
Mark 7:6-7

These same unbelievers were the ones who killed Jesus.
People of both types are walking the earth today. A deacon
at my church told me of how one day while at home
studying the word preparing to teach the singles' class the
upcoming Sunday, someone knocked on his door. He
thought that it was the man living above him coming down
to discuss the car he was looking into for my daughter. He
answered the door, but it was a gentleman from a cable
company looking to sell cable services. The guy was very
polite and asked if he was interrupting his dinner and the
deacon replied no, that he was just studying the word.
Because this young man had the first type of unbelief
where there was still a want of Christian faith, he asked the
deacon a question. He wanted to know the difference
between the trinity and the oneness of God. The deacon
witnessed to this young man and the gentleman was able to
leave there free of unbelief in this area.

But just like the Pharisees, there are people who will
not believe or put their trust in Christ no matter what. These
kinds of people are atheist. They completely lack a belief in
gods of any kind or supernatural beings like angels or
demons. I myself have never tried to understand where
their logic comes from but when I saw the movie *God's
Not Dead,* it opened my thoughts on how they may have
gotten that way. In the film, the philosophy professor who
wanted the students to denounce God was an atheist
because his mother had died. She was a Christian and as

such, he had prayed to God to heal her but she was not healed on this side of heaven. She was healed on the other side and he couldn't deal with it.

There are also those who just refuse to change from what they may have been taught. It amazes me how you can examine something in the bible with someone and lay it all down in scriptures, but their final words are, "well, this is what I was raised to believe and nothing is going to change that." This is rebellious. The word is very clear.

My people are destroyed for lack of knowledge: because thou hast rejected knowledge, I will also reject thee, that thou shalt be no priest to me: seeing thou hast forgotten the law of thy God, I will also forget thy children. Hosea 4:6

A couple of years ago I worked at Barnes & Noble. I had been there for over seven and a half years. During that time, several of us would sit down and talk about different things in the Bible. I have never worked in a place with so many different people of different religious backgrounds and denominations. There was me, Apostolic; my boss, AME; a co-worker, Catholic; another co-worker; Baptist; another co-worker, Church of God; yet another worker, Seventh-day Aventis; and then another co-worker who believed in Christ and in being a good person, but didn't go to church. Over the years we had some really good discussions about some truly deep beliefs. I'm the type of person that whenever I am approached with a subject or if someone gives me something contradictory to what I've been taught, I go back to the word to see what thus says the Lord. I found that over the years I had been on point with many of our topics like speaking in tongues, being baptized in Jesus' name, and the oneness of our

Savior. But because I had been so on point about so many things, so I thought, I had become arrogant.

But the Lord straightened me out one day, preventing arrogance from growing. The particular subject we were talking about was praise and worship. Once again, I believe in studying the word and going by what God has said, so as we were discussing this subject I found that I wasn't as knowledgeable as I had hoped and needed to be and I wasn't able to give my usual sound and rooted rebuttal to what was being said. I went home to study praise and worship and it was an eye opening experience for me.

Yes, I had been very confident and cocky about what I thought to be right because of having previously explained subjects, then having gone back to the word to confirm that I was really on point, but this particular time I was not. I was not necessarily wrong in my discussion with praise and worship, but the information that my coworker was giving to me was actually correct. I was not the expert I thought I was. I thank God for the opportunity to see it through that subject being discussed. I've always been told to study what the Bible says and to go from that because sometimes people teach you out of their traditions or teach you out of what they think to be the truth. Sometimes people teach or preach to you from a scripture but have completely transformed it to fit their own needs. This is exactly why I pray, seek God's face, and always go by the word. Even so, at Barnes & Noble I noticed that no matter how many times we would talk about certain subject matters, there was always one person who would not change or budge from his way of thinking. Regarding the second *unbelief* (not persuaded) where it talks about "without a Christian faith," we have to have faith that as we seek God's face, He will begin to reveal His mysteries to us. True, grandma may have taught us something at a young age, and yes, we may have grown up in a church where they believed such and such a thing but as God begins to reveal His mysteries to us, we get a better understanding of the truth that it is for us to change our way of thinking.

> *And be renewed in the spirit of your mind; And that ye put on the new man, which after God is created in righteousness and true holiness.* Ephesians 4:23-24

We then must conform to that newness of truth. We have to be filled with faith in our walk with God; we can't be so stubborn and hard-hearted that we can't be open minded to receive the things that God is trying to show us. There's tradition but God is more than tradition. There are beliefs that are rooted and grounded in scripture but once again, it may be that someone has taken that scripture and taught it according to how they wanted it to work for them in their situation. One of the major subjects I found that my coworker would not move on was "once saved, always saved," but this is not what God has said to us, His people.

There are two points that need to be driven home concerning unbelief, the first being the different types of unbelief. The second is that unbelief in any form is considered sin. Reconsider the definitions for both types of unbelief: *apistia* (not faithful) which means "faithlessness, disbelief (but a want of Christian faith), unfaithfulness (disobedience) – unbelief," and *apeitheia* (not persuaded) which means "disbelief (obstinate and rebellious) – disobedience, unbelief." Both words equally have disobedience in their core. When we have unbelief in our hearts, we are walking around in disobedience. There are several scriptures that use the word *unbelief* in one translation and *disobey* in another. This correlation is to say that unbelief is disobedience and vice versa.

For as ye in times past have not believed God, yet have now obtained mercy through their unbelief: Even so have these also now not believed, that through your mercy they also may obtain mercy. For God hath concluded them all in unbelief, that he might have mercy upon all. Romans 11:30-32

Just as you once were disobedient and failed to listen to God, but have now obtained mercy because of their disobedience, so they too have now become disobedient so that they too may one day receive mercy because of the mercy shown to you. For God has imprisoned all in disobedience so that He may show mercy to all [Jew and Gentile alike]. Romans 11:30-32 AMP

(v6) Seeing therefore it remaineth that some must enter therein, and they to whom it was first preached entered not in because of unbelief: (v 11) Let us labour therefore to enter into that rest, lest any man fall after the same example of unbelief. Hebrews 4:6,11

(v6) Therefore, since the promise remains for some to enter His rest, and those who formerly had the good news preached to them failed to [grasp it and did not] enter because of [their unbelief evidenced by] disobedience, (v11) Let us therefore make every effort to enter that rest [of God, to know and experience it for ourselves], so that no one will fall by following the same example of disobedience [as those who died in the wilderness]. Hebrews 4:6, 11 AMP

Unbelief in these scriptures is from the Greek word *apěithěia*. What is the Lord trying to tell us? Disobedience is sin.

> *For as by one man's disobedience many were made sinners, so by the obedience of one shall many be made righteous.* Romans 5:19

As I began to study this, I immediately had to repent for my unbelief because it is not my desire to walk in sin. In the index of my Bible, *sin* is stated as "disobeying God's law." Disobedience can be traced back to Adam and Eve. God told Adam not to eat of the tree of the knowledge of good and evil and he relayed that commandment to Eve. However, satan came in and convinced Eve to eat of the tree and she in turn persuaded Adam. Sin entered into the world because they disobeyed God's only law. Thus, if unbelief is disobedience and disobedience is sin, then unbelief is sin.

> *But the fearful, and unbelieving, and the abominable, and murderers, and whoremongers, and sorcerers, and idolaters, and all liars, shall have their part in the lake which burneth with fire and brimstone: which is the second death.* Revelation 21:8

We all have areas of unbelief that we need to convert to faith because unbelief will prevent us from seeing the mighty works of Christ.

> *And he did not many mighty works there because of their unbelief.* Matthew 13:58

Then came the disciples to Jesus apart, and said, Why could not we cast him out? And Jesus said unto them, Because of your unbelief: for verily I say unto you, If ye have faith as a grain of mustard seed, ye shall say unto this mountain, Remove hence to yonder place; and it shall remove; and nothing shall be impossible unto you. *Matthew 17:19-20*

Here is how we alter our unbelief into faith. Step one is to repent and have true repentance for the unbelief.

Repent ye therefore, and be converted, that your sins may be blotted out, when the times of refreshing shall come from the presence of the Lord. *Acts 3:19*

When we have true repentance, we are converted from the old man to the new man.

And be renewed in the spirit of your mind; And that ye put on the new man, which after God is created in righteousness and true holiness. *Ephesians 4:23-24*

The second step is to begin to read the word of God more, to memorize the word of God more, and to meditate on the word of God more. Once the word begins to live within the fiber of your being, the third and most crucial step is to be obedient to the word of God. Think about it. If unbelief is disobedience, then obedience breeds belief. To truly obey God's word means that you do what the word says to do in every situation you face in life. For example, if someone has mistreated you, you are being obedient to the word when you don't seek vengeance.

Dearly beloved, avenge not yourselves, but rather give place unto wrath: for it is written, Vengeance is mine; I will repay, saith the Lord. Romans 12:19

If you are looking for a way to avoid evil, you know to simply ask.

And I say unto you, Ask, and it shall be given you; seek, and ye shall find; knock, and it shall be opened unto you. For every one that asketh receiveth; and he that seeketh findeth; and to him that knocketh it shall be opened. Luke 11:9-10

Obedience is paying my tithes even though I don't have enough money to pay my bills because I know that the Lord will supply ALL of my needs.

But my God shall supply all your need according to his riches in glory by Christ Jesus. Philippians 4:19

No matter the situation, obey God's word for He will never steer you wrong. This is the only way to overcome unbelief.

Trust in the Lord with all thine heart; and lean not unto thine own understanding. In all thy ways acknowledge him, and he shall direct thy paths. Proverbs 3:5-6

Fear can keep us up all night long,

but faith makes one fine pillow.

Unknown

With Faith

Chapter 11

MY FEARS

For the majority of my life I have been afraid of all bugs, spiders, wasps and bees. I couldn't tell you where this fear came from, nor could I tell you why I was completely paralyzed from killing them. I am sure my husband would have wanted something that would help me get over this fear so he wouldn't have to be the bug killer in the house. My grandmother couldn't comprehend how I could be so much bigger than the bugs yet be such a baby when it came to trying to kill one. I'll never forget the day I was cleaning out the garage and spraying for spiders when I came across a huge one in the corner. I had the spray in my hand but couldn't bring myself to get close enough to the spider to spray it. My 79-year old grandmother had to come out into the garage to kill it.

As God began to deal with me on faith, He threw a curve ball into the game - fear. I was driving one day in mid-September returning to work from lunch with a very close coworker when I thought that something might have flown into my car. I remember very clearly telling my coworker that either something had flown by my window very closely or that it had flown into my car. It was our custom to stop at the mail box on our way back into the building so that she could retrieve the mail. As I turned to watch her get out of the car to check the mail, I saw a large wasp in my van on the back passenger window. To some that may have not been a big deal, but to me this was a huge thing. I was deathly afraid of wasps. It was worth throwing my car into park and jumping out. I didn't even look to see if any cars were coming. I just jumped out. There were two women nearby picking up their children from the bus stop. One of the women that was there used her son's backpack to get the wasp out. She could see my fear all over me.

About an hour later as I was driving to pick up my daughter, Camille, from school, when a circadian flew into my car. Just like the first time, I threw my car into park and jumped out. This time I was on a very busy stretch of road, but I still didn't pay any attention to see if vehicles were coming or not. I was so full of fear again that I just jumped out. Thank God that at that time there were no cars coming. Unlike the first time however, there was no one around to help me with the huge bug. I tried calling back to my job to have a young lady there come and get it out but no one answered the phone. I called several times but God had it orchestrated for me to deal with this on my own. It took me over 20 minutes to swat a dead circadian out of my car (it had died on impact when it hit my purse on the front passenger seat). My daughter had kept calling me to see where I was. She couldn't grasp the fear that had taken control over me in that moment.

I knew, after calming down, that God was trying to deal with me about my fear. Not just the fear of bugs, but fear in its totality. The very next day I was speaking to the First Lady of the church I was working at and God laid it on her heart to talk to me about her debilitating fear. She even said that she didn't know why she was telling me what she was telling me. I told her why. This prompted me to begin to study about fear and in my studying I found out that for every force and principle God has created, there existed a counterpoint. Fear is the counterpoint of faith. That's right, the complete opposite of faith is fear. This was an eye opening truth for me. It also let me know that God was about to do something amazing in my life.

I was just as sorely afraid of speaking in public as I was of bugs. I have no awareness of where this came from. For as long as I can remember, just the thought of having to speak in front of people would almost send me into a panic attack. The funny thing is, I had to take a public speaking class in college to get my degree. I just knew I was going to fail it. I had no false hopes of passing. Whenever I had to get up to give a speech, my hands would get sweaty and I felt like my heart was going to jump out of my chest. I would sit in my chair trying my best to calm my nerves so I wouldn't vomit in front of the class. I could never make my speech be as long as it needed to be to get an A on any one of them. Fear truly had me in the palm of its hands. It is only by the grace of the Lord that I did in fact pass. The class was only partially graded on the actual speeches, the rest came from tests and quizzes.

This fear of speaking in front of people has plagued me my whole life. One day I was asked to create a PowerPoint presentation that would be shared with the faculty and administration at the community college where I worked. I had no problem creating the slides and adding the information to be presented. On the day that I assumed my boss was going to present it, he said that I should do the presentation since I was familiar with the information. Immediately I went into a panic. My heart started racing and my palms started sweating. I could feel my blood pressure rising which caused me to have a headache. I felt like a dark blanket was being pulled over me; all I wanted to do was retreat and run away. My boss saw the physical changes happening right before his eyes and he allowed me to just sit in the room while he went through the slides and presented the information.

This fear and panic didn't just take place if I was to present to strangers. It took place every time I wanted to give a testimony at church. I would have to sit there from the beginning of service until the testimony portion and pump myself up. I would have to keep my breathing in check so that I wouldn't faint. I felt like my heart was going to beat out of my chest. There were many Sundays that I didn't win the fight against fear; I just sat there. Yes, I sat down on my testimony that would have glorified my Savior. It left me feeling defeated after church every time.

I vividly remember another instance when I had to speak at church. This time it wouldn't be from my pew in the congregation; it would be in the pulpit during our pastor's anniversary. I was the vice president of our church's Pastor's Aide Committee. It was customary for the president to end the anniversary service with closing remarks and to present the Pastor and First Lady with a love token, but the president was in the hospital with blood clots in his lungs. By him being in the hospital, that duty fell to me. It took everything in my being to walk up those steps, stand behind the podium and speak to the many people that had come out to celebrate my Pastor and First Lady. Even though I had written down everything that I wanted to say, fear came in and what should have been a heartfelt 2-3 minute thank you turned into a rapid-fire, 45-50 second blunder of appreciation. Then I ran out of the pulpit. Many people there encouraged my heart by letting me know that I had done a great job, but that I had just spoken way too fast. Still, those words did nothing to shake my fear.

I avoided speaking in the pulpit as much as I could but I did begin to give more testimonies in an attempt to battle this crippling feeling. Who would have known that I would have been asked to speak in front of people again? This time it wouldn't be just a 2-3 minute thank you, but a full-fledged 15-minute discourse on a topic. Evangelist Tara Jones asked me to speak during our Women's Fellowship for the month of October, 2013. I wasn't given the topic by the lovely Evang. Tara. I was just told to come however the Lord led me. I received this assignment in December of 2012 but kept denying the task until just about one month before I was scheduled to speak. Wanting to be obedient, I began to seek God for what He wanted me to speak about and that is when He gave me *faith* as well as *fear*. I completed the job with my head down almost the entire time. As stated in the introduction, it was a few weeks later that He told me to write a book.

It was only after I begun to write this book that Jesus truly began to deal patiently with me about my fears. In October of 2015, I was completely set free from the grip of fear during a women's conference. I was immediately put to the test about speaking, in front of a room full of strangers and I passed with flying colors. I am no longer bound by fear of bugs nor by fear of public speaking. The Lord let me know that He couldn't use me in that state. He needed me **fearless**.

Fear is born of satan, and if we would only take time to think a moment we would see that everything *satan says is founded upon a falsehood.*

A.B. Simpson

Chapter 12

FEAR BY SATAN

Just as belief is the first step towards trust then faith, doubt is the first step towards unbelief that could lead us to fear if not properly addressed. As of 2007, there were over 530 documented phobias. This tells me that we are not appropriately tackling fear. *Fear* as defined by the dictionary is:

1: frighten

2: to feel fear in (oneself)

3: to have a reverential awe of

4: to be afraid of: expect with alarm"[23]

There are two sides to the fear focus. One side is found in definition three, "a reverential awe," or as is often said, "fear of the Lord." Then there is the other side - all of the other meanings. We are going to start with these latter three then come back to the former. There are over ten variations for *fear* in the Hebrew and Greek Concordance. We are going to focus on the two main ones from the Hebrew (Old Testament) and Greek (New Testament). The first Hebrew word for *fear* is *yârê*, which means "morally to revere; causatively to frighten: - affright, be (make) afraid, dread (ful), (put in) fear (-ful, -fully, -ing), (be had in) reverence (end)."[24] *Fear* used in the New Testament comes from the Greek word *phŏbŏs* that can be defined as "(to be put in fear); alarm, or fright: - be afraid, exceedingly, fear, terror."[25]

> *For God hath not given us the spirit of fear; but of power, and of love, and of a sound mind.*
> II *Timothy 1:7*

If God did not give us this "spirit of fear," then who did? Going back to the Garden of Eden when satan beguiled Eve into eating from the tree, not only did doubt, unbelief, and sin enter into the world but so did fear.

> *And the Lord God called unto Adam, and said unto him, Where art thou? And he said, I heard thy voice in the garden, and I was afraid, because I was naked; and I hid myself.* Genesis *3:9-10*

Adam and Eve were afraid (fearful) to stand before God because they had become aware of their nakedness. Fear is a very destructive, crippling power. Being completely paralyzed by fear is why it took me over 20 minutes to get a dead circadian out of my car. Fear is destroying lives on a daily basis. Fear of being alone can cause men to kill their wives when they say they want a divorce. The same can be said for women allowing men to have complete and utter control over their lives; women can be riddled with the fear of not having someone to love them.

> *When your fear cometh as desolation, and your destruction cometh as a whirlwind; when distress and anguish cometh upon you.* Proverbs *1:27*

In studying fear, the Lord revealed to me that fear is so powerful that every time an angel or the Lord Himself would come to speak to a person, they would always have to say "fear not."

And, behold, an hand touched me, which set me upon my knees and upon the palms of my hands. And he said unto me, O Daniel, a man greatly beloved, understand the words that I speak unto thee, and stand upright: for unto thee am I now sent. And when he had spoken this word unto me, I stood trembling. Then said he unto me, Fear not, Daniel: for from the first day that thou didst set thine heart to understand, and to chasten thyself before thy God, thy words were heard, and I am come for thy words. Daniel 10:10-12

And there appeared unto him an angel of the Lord standing on the right side of the altar of incense. And when Zacharias saw him, he was troubled, and fear fell upon him. But the angel said unto him, Fear not, Zacharias: for thy prayer is heard; and thy wife Elisabeth shall bear thee a son, and thou shalt call his name John. Luke 1:11-13

And, lo, the angel of the Lord came upon them, and the glory of the Lord shone round about them: and they were sore afraid. And the angel said unto them, Fear not: for, behold, I bring you good tidings of great joy, which shall be to all people. For unto you is born this day in the city of David a Saviour, which is Christ the Lord. Luke 2:9-11

Before they could begin to comfort the person they had come down from heaven to minister to, they had to rebuke fear. Fear is the counterpoint of faith. That means fear is the complete opposite of faith, or that faith is on the far left end of the spectrum and fear is on the far right. Fear and faith cannot co-exist. One will always cancel the other out, so before an angel or the Lord could produce or elevate one's faith, they had to completely exterminate fear.

Fear is a spiritual force that has been perverted and twisted by satan himself. In chapter 9 it was discussed how doubt begins as a thought. There needs to be a deeper understanding of this. There is a Threefold Nature of Man; the body, the soul and the spirit. The body/soma is the flesh or carnal nature of a person.

> *And I, brethren, could not speak unto you as unto spiritual, but as unto carnal, even as unto babes in Christ. I have fed you with milk, and not with meat: for hitherto ye were not able to bear it, neither yet now are ye able. For ye are yet carnal: for whereas there is among you envying, and strife, and divisions, are ye not carnal, and walk as men?* 1 Corinthians 3:1-3

As we know, there are five senses that allow information to be brought from the outside world into our body. These five senses are gates to the body: sight, eye-gate; smell, nose-gate; hearing, ear-gate; taste, mouth-gate; and touch, feel-gate. The top two entry points of data into the body are the eye and ear gates. Because God loves us so much, He gave us instructions on these two gates.

> *My son, if thou wilt receive my words, and hide my commandments with thee; So that thou incline thine ear unto wisdom, and apply thine heart to understanding;* Proverbs 2:1-2

Let your eyes look directly ahead [toward the path of moral courage] And let your gaze be fixed straight in front of you [toward the path of integrity]. Proverbs 4:25 (AMP)

The soul/psyche is the mind, or natural nature of man.

But the natural man receiveth not the things of the Spirit of God: for they are foolishness unto him: neither can he know them, because they are spiritually discerned. 1 Corinthians 2:14

There are five cognitive portals from the body to the soul. These gateways are imagination, conscience, memory, reason, and affections. Doubt enters into the soul through thinking or reasoning. The thought may be, "if I pay my tithes, I won't have enough money to pay my bills." But this is also where memory of the scriptures kicks in.

I have been young, and now am old; yet have I not seen the righteous forsaken, nor his seed begging bread. Psalm 37:25

The spirit/pneuma or spiritual is the third nature of us humans. The heart is housed in this area. The Bible is quite unmistakable when it comes to the heart of those that are unfilled with the Holy Ghost.

The heart is deceitful above all things, and desperately wicked: who can know it? Jeremiah 17:9

And God saw that the wickedness of man was great in the earth, and that every imagination of the thoughts of his heart was only evil continually.

Genesis 6:5

O generation of vipers, how can ye, being evil, speak good things? for out of the abundance of the heart the mouth speaketh. Matthew 12:34

But when we are filled with the Holy Spirit, it comes into our hearts and causes us to be changed.

And because ye are sons, God hath sent forth the Spirit of his Son into your hearts, crying, Abba, Father. Galatians 4:6

Who hath also sealed us, and given the earnest of the Spirit in our hearts. 2 Corinthians 1:22

And you hath he quickened, who were dead in trespasses and sins; Wherein in time past ye walked according to the course of this world, according to the prince of the power of the air, the spirit that now worketh in the children of disobedience: Among whom also we all had our conversation in times past in the lusts of our flesh, fulfilling the desires of the flesh and of the mind; and were by nature the children of wrath, even as others. But God, who is rich in mercy, for his great love wherewith he loved us, Even when we were dead in sins, hath quickened us together with Christ, (by grace ye are saved;) And hath raised us up together, and made us sit together in heavenly places in Christ Jesus: Ephesians 2:1-6

The only access to the Spirit is through our will. This is exactly why God gave us free will.

And if it seem evil unto you to serve the Lord, choose you this day whom ye will serve; whether the gods which your fathers served that were on the other side of the flood, or the gods of the Amorites, in whose land ye dwell: but as for me and my house, we will serve the Lord. Joshua 24:15

A man's heart deviseth his way: but the Lord directeth his steps. Proverbs 16:9

For if we sin wilfully after that we have received the knowledge of the truth, there remaineth no more sacrifice for sins, Hebrews 10:26

As stated, fear and faith cannot co-exist in our heart. This is because fear is a spirit sent by the devil himself in an attempt to drive away the fruit of faith which is a manifestation of the Holy Spirit abiding in our hearts. Fear must be received before it can enter the heart and cancel out faith. Fear is fostered through meditating and acting on satan's lies. It pushes us into a level of emotion that often makes no sense at all. Meditating on fear is called worrying.

This book of the law shall not depart out of thy mouth; but thou shalt meditate therein day and night, that thou mayest observe to do according to all that is written therein: for then thou shalt make thy way prosperous, and then thou shalt have good success. Joshua 1:8

It would make sense that if we have to meditate on the word to be prosperous and have good success, then if we sit there and meditate on fear, it will begin to mature and cause us to act on it. Be careful not to take action based on a feeling that an evil spirit has dropped at our door, a feeling that very often has no reality at all.

Be careful for nothing: *Philippians 4:6 (a)*

Careful in this text of scripture means "worried." I like the Amplified Bible version because it breaks it down like this:

Do not fret or have anxiety about anything
Philippians 4:6 AMP(a)

Fear is NOT natural to the born-again believer because fear is of "the law of sin and death." We are of "the law of the Spirit of life."

There is therefore now no condemnation to them which are in Christ Jesus, who walk not after the flesh, but after the Spirit. For the law of the Spirit of life in Christ Jesus hath made me free from the law of sin and death. *Romans 8:1-2*

Our spirit/pneuma is either filled with the Holy Ghost and things of God, i.e. faith, worship, temperance, love, peace and meekness, or it is filled with unclean, demonic spirits. Ultimately, the choice is ours to make.

When the unclean spirit is gone out of a man, he walketh through dry places, seeking rest; and finding none, he saith, I will return unto my house whence I came out. And when he cometh, he findeth it swept and garnished. Then goeth he, and taketh to him seven other spirits more wicked than himself; and

they enter in, and dwell there: and the last state of that man is worse than the first. Luke 11:24-26

This is why the scripture is extremely clear about guarding our hearts.

Keep thy heart with all diligence; for out of it are the issues of life. *Proverbs 4:23*

David understood this and inquired of the Lord.

Create in me a clean heart, O God; and renew a right spirit within me. *Psalms 51:10*

We must daily ask God to search us.

Search me, O God, and know my heart: try me, and know my thoughts: And see if there be any wicked way in me, and lead me in the way everlasting. *Psalm 139:23-24*

In Matthew 4:1-10, when the devil came unto Jesus and attempted to pervert and twist the word of God, He spoke back to him the true, unadulterated word of God. We have to do the same thing, speaking back to satan what the word says about whatever situation he is attempting to entwine us in with his lies. And just like he fled after Jesus stood flat footed against him, the spirit of fear has no choice but to flee when we speak against it.

Ye are of God, little children, and have overcome them: because greater is he that is in you, than he that is in the world. *1 John 4:4*

For the word of God is quick, and powerful, and sharper than any twoedged sword, piercing even to the dividing asunder of soul and spirit, and of the joints and marrow, and is a discerner of the thoughts and intents of the heart. Hebrews 4:12

To completely annihilate and wipe out fear, we need love. Where the Holy Ghost reigns, fear has to flee. If you are filled with the Holy Ghost, you are going to be filled with God's love.

That Christ may dwell in your hearts by faith; that ye, being rooted and grounded in love, May be able to comprehend with all saints what is the breadth, and length, and depth, and height; And to know the love of Christ, which passeth knowledge, that ye might be filled with all the fulness of God. Ephesians 3:17-19

There is no fear in love; but perfect love casteth out fear: because fear hath torment. He that feareth is not made perfect in love. 1 John 4:18

Once you have completely removed fear from you, DO NOT allow the devil to return to you with it. I remember one time after I had been delivered from fear, satan tried to come at me again with it. I had to remind him that I was freed from fear and he needed to back off. Remember, greater is He that is in you than he that is the world.

For ye have not received the spirit of bondage again to fear, but ye have received the Spirit of adoption, whereby we cry, Abba, Father. Romans 8:15

The only God-ordained fear is the fear of God, and if we fear Him, we don't have to fear anyone or anything else.

Mark Batterson

With Faith

Chapter 13

FEAR OF THE LORD

On the other side of the fear coin is what can be called a good fear. Some discussion is needed on this flip side of the coin to ensure that the devil doesn't use his fear to keep us from the right fear. This *fear* comes from the third definition given by Merriam-Webster, "reverential awe." This *fear* also comes from the Hebrew word *yah'âh* which means "fear (also as infinitive); morally reverence."[24] When the scriptures state "the fear of the Lord," they are referring to this type of fear. Not a fear where we are to be morbidly afraid of God, but a "reverential" fear. God is our friend but He is also our sovereign Lord and for that fact alone we are to always have a reverential fear of Christ. When we have a fear of the Lord, it is the beginning of wisdom. Just like belief is the first step to faith, reverence is the first step to understanding.

> *The fear of the Lord is the beginning of knowledge:*
> *but fools despise wisdom and instruction.* Proverbs 1:7

When we fear the Lord we will hate evil. The scriptures are abundantly clear that we cannot serve both God and the devil so we must either fear God, love Him, and fulfill His plans for us, or be a slave to the devil.

> *The fear of the Lord is to hate evil: pride, and*
> *arrogancy, and the evil way, and the froward mouth,*
> *do I hate.* Proverbs 8:13

No man can serve two masters: for either he will hate the one, and love the other; or else he will hold to the one, and despise the other. Ye cannot serve God and mammon. Matthew 6:24

It is everyone's desire to live a rich and bountiful life. Rich does not necessarily always refer to money. In this instance rich is meant to describe a fertile life lived to its fullest potential, not a life abruptly cut short. It was quite surprising to find out that to have a reverential fear of the Lord allows us access to a fountain of life.

The fear of the Lord is a fountain of life, to depart from the snares of death. Proverbs 14:27

But whosoever drinketh of the water that I shall give him shall never thirst; but the water that I shall give him shall be in him a well of water springing up into everlasting life. John 4:14

I am come that they might have life, and that they might have it more abundantly. John 10:10(b)

The Bible is full of examples of great men and women who feared the Lord. Here are just a few:

- Noah - *By faith Noah, being warned of God of things not seen as yet, moved with fear, prepared an ark to the saving of his house; by the which he condemned the world, and became heir of the righteousness which is by faith.* Hebrews 11:7

Read Noah's entire story in Genesis 6:8-9:29.

- Abraham - *And he said, Lay not thine hand upon the lad, neither do thou any thing unto him: for now I know that thou fearest God, seeing thou hast not withheld thy son, thine only son from me.* Genesis 22:12

Read Abraham's entire story in Genesis 11:27-25:18.

- Job – *And the Lord said unto Satan, Hast thou considered my servant Job, that there is none like him in the earth, a perfect and an upright man, one that feareth God, and escheweth evil?* Job 1:8

Read his entire story in the book of Job.

- Nehemiah – *But the former governors that had been before me were chargeable unto the people, and had taken of them bread and wine, beside forty shekels of silver; yea, even their servants bare rule over the people: but so did not I, because of the fear of God.* Nehemiah 5:15

Read his entire story in the book of Nehemiah.

- Joseph – *And Joseph said unto them the third day, This do, and live; for I fear God.* Genesis 42:18

Read Joseph's entire story in Genesis 37:1-50:26.

- Obadiah - *And Ahab called Obadiah, which was the governor of his house. (Now Obadiah feared the Lord greatly: For it was so, when Jezebel cut off the prophets of the Lord, that Obadiah took an hundred prophets, and hid them by fifty in a cave, and fed them with bread and water.) 1 Kings 18:3-4*

Read his entire story in the book Obadiah.

•   David – *But as for me, I will enter Your house through the abundance of Your steadfast love and tender mercy; At Your holy temple I will bow [obediently] in reverence for You. Psalm 5:7 (AMP)*

Read David's entire story in I Samuel 15:1-I Kings 2:11.

•   Initial Christians - *Then had the churches rest throughout all Judaea and Galilee and Samaria, and were edified; and walking in the fear of the Lord, and in the comfort of the Holy Ghost, were multiplied. Acts 9:31*

Jeremiah posed a question, "Who would not fear thee, O King of nations?" I pose that same question to you. Who would not fear the mighty, one and only King of kings, Lord of lords, Alpha and Omega, the Great I Am?

Who would not fear thee, O King of nations? for to thee doth it appertain: forasmuch as among all the wise men of the nations, and in all their kingdoms, there is none like unto thee. Jeremiah 10:7

For the Lord your God dried up the waters of Jordan from before you, until ye were passed over, as the Lord your God did to the Red sea, which he dried up from before us, until we were gone over: That all the people of the earth might know the hand of the Lord,

that it is mighty: that ye might fear the Lord your
God for ever. Joshua 4:23-24

To fear the Lord is completely and utterly the opposite of the kind of fear the enemy attempts to bring to us. We are to fear or reverence Christ and reject any fear that is dropped at our feet. One last thought:

Now therefore fear the Lord, and serve him in
sincerity and in truth: and put away the gods which
your fathers served on the other side of the flood, and
in Egypt; and serve ye the Lord. And if it seem evil
unto you to serve the Lord, choose you this day
whom ye will serve; whether the gods which your
fathers served that were on the other side of the
flood, or the gods of the Amorites, in whose land ye
dwell: but as for me and my house, we will serve the
Lord. Joshua 24:14-15

You can't stand effectively on "blind" faith.

You must have a **"knowing" faith,** *and that comes from believing wholeheartedly what the Word promises. You know God has spoken it and declared it to be so, and you know you can depend on that.*

God's Keys to Life
Gloria Copeland

Chapter 14

With Faith

In chapter 2 we discussed what faith is. As a refresher, faith is the confident assurance in Jesus Christ that the things we have hope for are going to happen and are evident, even though we have not seen it yet. Faith is perceiving as real fact what is not yet revealed to the senses. Also pointed out was that we all have been given a measure of faith because without faith it is impossible to please God. If it is impossible to please Him without faith, just consider how pleased He is when we use our faith.

We can read throughout the Bible what faith has done for so many people. The centurion's servant was healed because the centurion had such great faith. Jesus was so delighted by his faith that He never actually made it to the house to say, "servant, thy master's faith has made thee whole," nor did He say to the friends, "return home the servant is healed." All He said was, "I have not found so great faith, no, not in Israel." Jesus was so overjoyed at seeing this level of faith that He didn't have to physically go and lay hands on the servant. He just did what was being asked of Him, right from where He stood. Just think how Jesus would act if we asked something of Him and activated our faith to receive it. Not asking then doubting or having a backup plan, but just standing on faith.

Now when he had ended all his sayings in the audience of the people, he entered into Capernaum.

And a certain centurion's servant, who was dear unto him, was sick, and ready to die. And when he heard of Jesus, he sent unto him the elders of the Jews, beseeching him that he would come and heal his servant. And when they came to Jesus, they besought him instantly, saying, That he was worthy for whom he should do this: For he loveth our nation, and he hath built us a synagogue. Then Jesus went with them. And when he was now not far from the house, the centurion sent friends to him, saying unto him, Lord, trouble not thyself: for I am not worthy that thou shouldest enter under my roof: Wherefore neither thought I myself worthy to come unto thee: but say in a word, and my servant shall be healed. For I also am a man set under authority, having under me soldiers, and I say unto one, Go, and he goeth; and to another, Come, and he cometh; and to my servant, Do this, and he doeth it. When Jesus heard these things, he marvelled at him, and turned him about, and said unto the people that followed him, I say unto you, I have not found so great faith, no, not in Israel. And they that were sent, returning to the house, found the servant whole that had been sick. Luke 7:1-10

What about the woman with an issue of blood? We have all heard the story, but have you taken the time to dissect it? Here was a woman who had a blood condition that no doctor could say what it was. She had this condition for 12 years and had spent all the money that she possessed. She hadn't gotten any better; in fact, she had gotten worse. She had heard about Jesus and all the miracles He was performing. She didn't say to herself that she needed to get

His attention somehow so He could heal her; she knew that if she could just touch a piece of his garment (just the hem), that she would no longer have to be plagued by this undiagnosed condition. The scriptures let us know that without Jesus even being aware of her presence, she was made whole by her faith. Two points for consideration. First, if Jesus being wrapped in flesh had enough power that she was healed by faith from just touching the hem of His garment, how much more power does He have now, being wrapped in glory? Secondly, if she was made whole by just her faith connecting with His garment without Jesus knowing that she was in need, then how much more will He do now, being omniscient (all knowing), when we connect our faith with Him?

And a certain woman, which had an issue of blood twelve years, And had suffered many things of many physicians, and had spent all that she had, and was nothing bettered, but rather grew worse, When she had heard of Jesus, came in the press behind, and touched his garment. For she said, If I may touch but his clothes, I shall be whole. And straightway the fountain of her blood was dried up; and she felt in her body that she was healed of that plague. And Jesus, immediately knowing in himself that virtue had gone out of him, turned him about in the press, and said, Who touched my clothes? And his disciples said unto him, Thou seest the multitude thronging thee, and sayest thou, Who touched me? And he looked round about to see her that had done this thing. But the woman fearing and trembling, knowing what was done in her, came and fell down before him, and told him all the truth. And he said unto her, Daughter, thy faith hath made thee whole; go in peace, and be whole of thy plague. Mark 5:25-34

With faith we are justified. *Justification* or *justified* means "to render, show or regard as just or innocent; to be causatively make right in a moral sense – cleanse or cleared of guilt." To better understand, by our faith that we have in Christ Jesus, we are now declared to be guilt free, or righteous (right standing with God).

Whom God hath set forth to be a propitiation through faith in his blood, to declare his righteousness for the remission of sins that are past, through the forbearance of God; To declare, I say, at this time his righteousness: that he might be just, and the justifier of him which believeth in Jesus. Romans 3:25-26

Being considered just, we can't live without faith. The Bible is extremely clear on how the just are to live. We are to live with faith in Jesus that He will (among other things): order your footsteps, lead and guide you in His righteousness, word your mouth when witnessing to others, give the increase when you sow a seed into someone's life, and keep you in His perfect peace when you leave home for the day. We live with faith.

For therein is the righteousness of God revealed from faith to faith: as it is written, The just shall live by faith. Romans 1:17

Behold, his soul which is lifted up is not upright in him: but the just shall live by his faith. Habakkuk 2:4

But that no man is justified by the law in the sight of God, it is evident: for, The just shall live by faith.
Galatians 3:11

In Romans, Paul lets us know that we are "being justified freely by his grace" (Romans 3:24), and that "a man is justified by faith" (Romans 3:28). These verses can seem to be contradictory but they are not. Just like Channel 4 is the station you turn your TV to when you want to watch the program *NCIS*, faith is the channel to get us to the source of grace. So with faith we have access to His grace.

Therefore being justified by faith, we have peace with God through our Lord Jesus Christ: By whom also we have access by faith into this grace wherein we stand, and rejoice in hope of the glory of God.
Romans 5:1-2

We know that we are to put on our whole armor of God. This is laid out for us in Ephesians 6:10-17. But what I found quite interesting is that when it comes to verse 16, it starts off "above all." *Above all* means "especially, in particular or most of all." That lets me know that this part of the armor is extremely important: it is the shield of faith. With the shield of faith, we will be able to resist evil and quench all the fiery darts of the wicked. The whole armor of God is important; each component has a specific job to do by protecting a certain area of the body. The breastplate protects the vital organs (the heart), and the helmet is covers the head (the mind). These pieces are stationary; they are unable to move. The shield, however, is portable and able to move freely. It can assist the helmet and protect the head, or it can assist the breastplate and protect the body. It can also provide protection for the uncovered and exposed parts of the body. In addition, the shield is a shield of *faith* because the word informs us that our faith overcomes the world.

> *For whatsoever is born of God overcometh the world: and this is the victory that overcometh the world, even our faith. 1 John 5:4*

We walk with faith and not by sight. Despite the news stories about recession, we walk with faith trusting and knowing that the Lord will supply all of our needs. Regardless of the number of planes that have crashed over the years, we walk with faith knowing that when we are on an aircraft it will land at its destination without incident. In the face of my lack of education and experience, I walk with faith knowing that the promotion I am seeking belongs to me. Notwithstanding all the hell that is going on around us, we walk with faith standing on God's word that as long as we keep our minds stayed on Him, He will keep us in perfect peace. With faith, our outlook is completely different. It's like having on a pair of eyeglasses that allows you to see the supernatural instead of the natural.

> *For we walk by faith [we regulate our lives and conduct ourselves by our conviction or belief respecting man's relationship to God and divine things, with trust and holy fervor; thus we walk] not by sight or appearance. 2 Corinthians 5:7 AMP*

With faith, our prayers will be answered. This is not to say that whatever we ask for in prayer will be given to us, because some things might not be God's will for us. But if we pray with faith asking for those things that are in His perfect will, we shall receive.

And whatever you ask for in prayer, having faith and [really] believing, you will receive. Matthew 21:22 AMP

That Christ may dwell in your hearts by faith; that ye, being rooted and grounded in love, May be able to comprehend with all saints what is the breadth, and length, and depth, and height; And to know the love of Christ, which passeth knowledge, that ye might be filled with all the fulness of God. Ephesians 3:17-19

In order for us to know the totality of God - His breadth, His length, His depth and His height, we have to operate in faith. Faith is the only key to unlock the mysteries of God. If we don't have faith, we will never be able to grasp all that He has in store for us. We must breath, eat and sleep faith. There is no other option.

Faith isn't faith

until it's all you're holding on to.

Unknown

Chapter 15

TIFFANY'S TESTIMONY

Tiffany Taylor, a friend of mine for many years, truly blessed me and helped me to elevate my faith when I heard her testimony of her faith walk. In 2004, she was working at Washington University in St. Louis, MO, and loved her job there. She went on maternity leave at the end of 2004 with her second child, Matthew. While she was on leave she received a call from a friend and former coworker, Jackie, from Barnes Jewish Hospital (at that time they were both medical assistants). Jackie called her to tell her that she knew of a job at St. Louis University. A manager there was looking for a great medical assistant to work with the head doctor in the gastroenterology (GI) department, and Jackie had recommended her for the position.

Jackie and Tiffany had attended the same college, studying to receive their degree as medical assistants (MAs). Jackie graduated about two years after Tiffany. After Jackie's graduating, they began working together at Barnes Hospital and Tiffany was her preceptor (trainer). Tiffany was the one who oriented her into her position and Jackie became an excellent medical assistant.

During the call, Jackie was telling Tiffany all about this wonderful job. At first Tiffany was unsure because she was only on maternity leave and she truly loved her job at Washington University. Since Jackie had submitted Tiffany's name for this position at SLU, Tiffany started receiving calls from the manager, Kelvin Barnes. He would leave Tiffany messages saying that Jackie had recommended her to them and that they were looking for a really strong medical assistant to work with Dr. Bacon, the head of GI. He explained that he greatly needed someone who was strong because he had lost a lot of MAs and that Jackie said that she, Tiffany, would be perfect for the job. He also told her that she could name her price and that they would negotiate her salary to pay her want she wanted.

As Tiffany was toiling in her mind over what to do, she thought about everything. She was very content at her job and was making pretty good money. Her pay in 2004 was $11.00 an hour, which was on the higher end for an MA at the time. She said to herself that one way to see how serious they were would be to ask for $13.50 an hour. She realized that this was high pay and she thought they probably wouldn't give it to her. So she asked. Guess what? Kelvin agreed to pay her that salary rate. She returned to Washington University after maternity leave and put in her two-week notice.

Tiffany began working at SLU on Monday, February 14, 2005. She was working there, making the money that she wanted, and she loved the patients and the doctor she was working for. She was also working with her friend, Jackie. But there was a registered nurse there that was downright mean and nasty. Tiffany could see now why they had lost so many MAs and now needed a strong one. Even so, she was enjoying her job working with friends and being in an office that was fun, but she also had to work one-to-one with this nurse. Tiffany had her own office but still had to interact with this nurse quite a bit throughout the day. Once she saw how strong of an MA Tiffany was, the nurse began to put a lot of her work on her. The nurse, who seemed as if she were sitting around doing nothing, began taking all the credit for the nursing work that Tiffany was actually completing. After working at the clinic for 11 months, Tiffany decided she needed to find another job and she gave her two-week notice.

While working at SLU, she received the precious gift of the Holy Ghost on July 3, 2005. Thank you, Lord! Now being filled with the Holy Ghost and having such a close relationship with God, she began to seek Him about what she should do concerning her working at SLU. She prayed and prayed but for what seemed to be the longest time, she didn't get an answer from the Lord. She decided since she had not heard anything from God that she would stay the course and remain at SLU.

In December of 2005, Tiffany began to feel in her spirit, "Ok, it's time for you to quit." She was thinking that she didn't have another job, so she needed to find one. She thought that this was the Lord finally releasing her from her job at SLU and from working with this nurse. Because Tiffany is a planner, she believes in doing things decently and in order so she began to look for another job. As she was looking, she didn't find anything comparable to SLU or even to Washington University. She remained at SLU and kept looking but God was still saying to her, "You need to quit." Tiffany was still quite new in her relationship with the Lord and she had never heard Him like this before. She just assumed that the right job was just around the corner. She kept looking for a job and kept working, but things in the office with the nurse went from uncomfortable to unbearable and from bad to a whole lot worse. The nurse's attitude became dreadful but Tiffany had never quit a job before without having another one lined up. On top of all this, she had two little ones at home to consider.

Things were continually getting worse and the Lord was speaking to her louder and louder, so she put in her two-week notice without having another job in tow. She decided to take a leap of faith and trust that what God was telling her to do was in His perfect plan for her life and that He had something else for her. While she did put in her two-week notice in faith, she didn't wait to hear from the Lord concerning what she was to do next. Frantically she looked for another job and found a temporary agency that would pay her the same pay that she was making at SLU, but she would have to work at various locations. She decided that this would be good enough until she found permanent work. She believed that this was in God's plan for her because she was hired two days before her two weeks were up.

She stopped working at SLU on a Friday and began working for the agency the following Monday. Her first assignment was at a clinic where she was told that her primary job would be drawing blood. She felt very confident that this placement would be a good fit because one of her strengths was phlebotomy. Day one came, and she was told that all blood draws in her area would be sent to her but she only received one person. Subsequently, she sat around all day doing nothing, which was very difficult for Tiffany, being the outgoing, hard-working person that she is. She called the agency that evening to let them know that this assignment was not for her and that she needed something faster paced. But they told her to give it another day as they had just heard from the clinic. They said they loved Tiffany and had given the agency only a good report.

Tiffany did what was asked of her and returned the following day. But in her spirit God was saying to her, "This is not your job." Hearing this, she didn't want to waste her time at the clinic, or anywhere that wasn't the place God had for her. Once again she called the agency at the end of the day to inform them that this assignment was not for her. In speaking with her recruiter about the placement, the recruiter got upset. She felt that there was no way Tiffany could know that this was not a good post for her after only two days. While the recruiter's displeasure should have been a red flag to her, Tiffany was holding on to her faith that when God said it wasn't for her, there was no need to return. She knew He had something better out there for her.

Reluctantly they gave Tiffany another placement and it was at Washington University. That's right. Her second placement was at her old job at Wash U. Here she was saying to herself, "Go figure; just like God." Nevertheless, after working for a few days she felt an unrest and uneasiness in her spirit. She began to pray, "God, what is it that you want me to do? I know this is not what you have for me." She prayed and prayed and completely sought the face of Christ and He said to her in an audible voice, "I told you to quit!" While some people may say they have never heard the voice of the Lord, Tiffany declares that there were two very prominent instances in her life when she has heard the audible voice of God, and this was one of them. He was telling her, "I told you to quit!" There was no point in her returning to the agency and indeed, she didn't. Tiffany was going over the details of what had occurred with a friend and during the conversation her friend began to ask her what it was that God wanted her to do. Her response was that she didn't know; all she knew was that it wasn't working these jobs. The friend reminded Tiffany that when they were working together at SLU, Tiffany told her that she was performing the duties of the nurse, so maybe she should go to nursing school to become a nurse since she was doing all of the nurse's work anyway, and doing it quite well. Immediately after her friend made that statement, all Tiffany could hear was bells and whistles going off in her head. She didn't hear anything else her friend was saying for a few moments. This was it. That was what God wanted her to do. She had received the revelation.

Now that she had received the revelation to become a nurse, Tiffany knew that she had to begin the search for the correct program. It had been years since she was in school, and having been raised in Missouri but now living in Belleville, IL, she was not quite sure what school to attend. The Lord began to direct her path and He directed her to Southwestern Illinois College in Belleville, IL. She didn't know much about the college and in fact, the only thing she did know was that her sister-in-law was attempting to get into the nursing program there. Tiffany wasted no time; she began to look into the nursing program at SWIC. The very next week she went to take her entrance exam for the college and they were able to give her the results immediately for the classes she tested into. Normally a student would have to take additional math classes to build up to the math class for the nursing program, but Christ being Christ, and Tiffany being obedient and stepping out on faith even though she was not a good student in math during high school, she tested into the lowest passing math level that was required for the nursing program. There were no additional classes needed. Tiffany received her revelation towards the end of January/beginning of February, 2006. Classes had already started on all campuses in the local area including at SWIC. But because the Lord had ordained this, every class that she needed was offered as a mid-semester course. Instead of having to sit out until the next semester began in the summer, she was able to start all of her classes in March. The way the nursing program usually worked, you applied in September to be accepted in April to begin the classes in August. In addition, there were certain classes that had to be taken before applying, but there were some you could be enrolled

With Faith

in when applying just by "guestimating" what your grade would be based on other classes taken. Tiffany was able to take three classes in the spring semester and three classes in the summer semester, which only left three classes needed towards her pre-requisites for the nursing program. Look at God!!

Like any nursing program in the world, it is cut throat to get in and spaces are limited. It was no different at Southwestern Illinois College. At this college, those students with straight A's automatically get in and if there are any spaces left they begin to admit those with B's, and so on. With the help of the Lord, Tiffany was able to make all A's in the six classes she had taken up to her applying for the program. One of the classes she had taken was chemistry. With physics being her major in high school, Tiffany never had taken a chemistry class; nevertheless, she got an A at SWIC.

Everyone she had talked to kept telling her not to apply for the program because she had just started at SWIC and wouldn't get in; they said she should wait until the following year. Tiffany obeyed the Lord and ignored the crowd, "guestimated" the grades she would obtain in her last three classes, received all A's in them, and applied for the nursing program in September, 2006.

Her sister-in-law had applied to the nursing program the year prior and was not accepted because she had a couple of C's, but at this point they were now both applying to the program. April came around and they were both waiting to see who got in. The nursing program had seats for 83 people; 276 people applied. That meant that only 30% of the people that applied would be allowed entrance into this lucrative program. Tiffany was accepted after only being at the college for three semesters while her sister-in-law was rejected once again. She knew that this was God's plan because everything came together in her favor and went smoothly. This is not to say that it wasn't hard; in fact, it was. Nonetheless, she did all she could do and put the rest into God's hands. Mind you, she was married with two children and had a lot going on in her marriage but God was really sustaining her and helping her through.

Tiffany was able to go through the nursing program without taking a semester off or being dropped from the program. The program was so intense that if you received a C in a class, you would be put out of the program and would have to sit out until that class came around again the next year. She was able to get all prerequisites done within that first year and was able to start the program and classes. During the program, the students perform clinicals. Clinicals are when you actually go into the hospitals and follow nurses to get the practicum of applying what you are learning in the classroom to real life situations. As we all know, hospitals never close. Clinical are scheduled at various local hospitals in the area up to a 50-mile range and at any time when you are not in class. They are required, or you will be terminated from the program.

One semester she received a letter while on break stating that clinicals would be on Wednesday nights for the upcoming semester; this is Tiffany's bible study night at church. She prayed and had the saints come together in agreement and pray that the Lord would move on her behalf about this matter. She knew that if God was doing this for her, there was no way that He wanted to take her out of services. She told God, "I know as faithful as You have been to me, You do not want me to miss out on service." Tiffany and her fellow church members prayed continually. Two weeks later when the semester began, she received a new letter apologizing that for some unforeseen circumstances, clinicals would not be on Wednesday nights

With Faith

but instead on Tuesday nights. Tiffany knew that this was the Lord's doing because she had remained faithful to Him.

In December of 2008, she began to work at St. Elizabeth's Hospital as a student nurse. She was working in obstetrics (OB), and due to her diligence and excellent work ethics, her boss offered her a job at the hospital upon her graduation. Everyone just knew that she would accept the job and work there. Tiffany was able to go through nursing school and graduate in 2009 at the top of her class. She was the president of the Student Nursing Association, which was a historical moment because she was the first African American at SWIC to ever hold that title. At the time of graduation, St. Elizabeth's Hospital had a program for new nurses where they would start you off working a rotating shift. This meant you would have to work some nights, days and evenings. Tiffany knew that this wasn't what God had for her. She was looking for a Monday through Friday day shift job. She had two small children in school and those hours would work very well with their schedule. She knew that she couldn't work rotating shifts because there would be some Wednesday nights that she would have to work, as well as Sundays, which meant that she would be taken away from church and have to miss out on those services. Tiffany just truly believed that if God had blessed her to make it through the nursing program, He would bless her with the job that she desired. A nurse who was saved told her that she was being too picky and that as a new nurse she had to take whatever she could get. She said that Tiffany was already working at a dream job with a good hospital and that she needed to remain there because God would understand if you missed church. Despite having a saved nurse telling her this, Tiffany stood on faith and said, "NO. I know what I want and I believe that my

Lord and Savior Jesus Christ will give me the desires of my heart. He has kept me this far and will not leave me now."

Tiffany graduated in May and took her state board exam on July 3, 2009. She passed and was hired by Southern Illinois Healthcare Foundation. The job she got was a job that in the posting stated they would only hire nurses with prior nursing experience and only nurses with a Bachelor's degree. Here was Tiffany, no RN experience, just having passed the boards, and only holding an Associate's degree in Nursing. Don't tell me what God can't do. The job was Monday through Friday, day shift, and she was working with pediatrics which is what she loved doing. This was truly a blessing from the Lord.

God is truly good all the time. He has blessed her career tremendously. She stayed at Southern Illinois Healthcare Foundation Mother & Child Center for the first three years of her nursing career. While pregnant with their third child, Tiffany wanted to be able to be home during the day with her children. She prayed and sought the Lord's face once again continuously. It was her desire to be able to be home for her children and husband. Once again, Jesus came through. Upon returning to work after maternity leave, she was able to start a job where she worked 12-hour shifts on Friday, Saturday, and Sunday nights. This worked out for her in so many ways. Like as most churches have decided to do, her church no longer held service on Sunday evenings. This new job allowed her to be there during the week for her family and not miss any services.

She knows that the Lord has ordained her career in nursing. Fast forward to today. On September 6th of 2014, we were both in one of our good friend's wedding. This is another testimony in itself. Tiffany was satisfied in her career. She was making more now than ever before. All things were well. She was content where she was financially, career wise, and wasn't even thinking about making any career moves. She just knew that she would retire doing what she was doing. Oh, but God had another plan. As she was sitting at the head table during the wedding reception dinner, another one of the women who was in the wedding party was seated next to her. Her name is Catherine Marshall. Catherine is a powerful woman of God and is on the rise in her ministry. Catherine began to reveal to Tiffany some things of the Lord. She let Tiffany know that God had more for her; He didn't want her to stay where she was as a nurse. Tiffany had a funny look on her face because she was perplexed. She questioned Catherine and asked if she was sure this was for her. Catherine reassured her and continued to let her know what God was saying for her. She also told her if she planned to go forward in nursing, to check out Southern Illinois University Edwardsville. That is where Catherine went and they have a great MSN Nurse Practitioner program. Tiffany was sitting there but not really digesting it. She was actually content where she was in her life, but being saved she knew if the Lord said it, He would send confirmation.

One night while at work Tiffany decided just to look into the program offered at SIUE. She had not received confirmation yet, but she wanted to satisfy this curiosity. She began looking into the program and pricing and was astonished at the discounted price for nurses. She was so amazed that she actually called her husband, Brandon, in the middle of the night to tell him how much of a savings it was for nurses. Tiffany printed out the forms to mail off to get more information. But by the end of the week she had not mailed them. Upon returning to work the following Friday, September 20th, she received an email from work stating that the company, SSM, had started a bridging program for their RNs to bridge into a one year BSN that would then allow them to bridge into the MSN-Nurse Practitioner program, and that they had started a partnership with SIUE. First off, Tiffany had not shared what Catherine had told her with anyone other than Brandon. Secondly, this was the same program that Catherine told her to look into, the one she had just looked at the week prior. Finally, the program would be discounted even more going through her job and the company would even pay for a nice size chunk of the tuition. On top of that, she would not have to pay anything out of pocket because SSM would pay everything up front and just do a payroll deduction for what they didn't cover. This was her confirmation! This is a great example. When God has something for you, it is just for you, and He will open doors and make ways for you to obtain it. He is so great and greatly to be praised!

In January 2015, Tiffany began embarking on her journey as she advances in her nursing career. It took some getting used to, the new schedule and the change of going back to school now with four children, the youngest being 15 months old. But she has said, "I notice that the times in my life when things seem to be completely chaotic are the times when I lean and depend most on God." We know that this is exactly what He wants, for us to be totally dependent and reliant on Him. She can now see the things that He has been doing in her life. It's been six years since she graduated from SWIC with her nursing degree. Tiffany hadn't seen the inside of a college since then and now most of her classmates are 10-15 years younger than her. But so far she has aced every quiz and test with the help of the Lord. She is so thankful to Him and she knows that He is in the midst of this all.

The Lord showed me a big red door. On the other side I could hear people having a good time. It was as if there were a party going on.

But it wasn't really a party.

He was showing me what I envision joy, peace, and happiness to be. The big red door was locked and I was holding a gold colored key.

While listening to the joy, peace, and happiness on the other side of the door, *the Lord let me know* that the key I was holding was faith.

He told me that faith is the key that would unlock that door. All I had to do was use it. *With faith*, we have the key to unlock the door to obtain whatever is on the other side.

Endnotes

1. Merriam-Webster. *Faith.* n.d. Merriam-Webster.com. October 2013.

2. Kadlec, Charles. *The Rising Price Of the Falling Dollar.* 19 March 2012. http://www.forbes.com/sites/charleskadlec/2012/03/19/the-rising-price-of-the-falling-dollar/. 18 September 2013.

3. Sivy, Michael. *Can the U.S. Dollar Become Almighty Once Again?* 20 March 2013. September 18 2013. <http://business.time.com/2013/03/20/can-the-u-s-dollar-become-almighty-once-again/#ixzz2fExGlxmh>.

4. Strong, James LL.D, S.T.D. "New Strong's Concise Dictionary of the Words in the Greek Testament." *The New Strong's Exhaustive Concordance of the Bible.* Nashville: Thomas Nelson, Inc., Publishers, 1995. 71. Book.

5. Ibid., 45.

6. Ibid., 46.

7. Ibid., 24.

8. Ibid., 25.

9. Ibid., 98.

10. Merriam-Webster. *Believe.*

11. Cree, Chris. *Purposely Different: The Difference Between Faith and Belief.* 2011. https://purposelydifferent.com/the-difference-between-faith-and-belief/. 2013.

12. Strong, 55.

13. Ibid., 102.

14. Barnes, Albert. "Barnes' Notes Psalm 119." 2004-2014.
    Bible Hub.
    http://biblehub.com/commentaries/barnes/psalms/119.htm.
    March 2014.

15. *The New Open Bible Study Edition.* Nashville: Thomas
    Nelson, Inc. Publishers, 1990. Bible.

16. Merriam-Webster. *Destabilized.*

17. Ibid., *Diversion.*

18. Ibid., *Division.*

19. Ibid. *Discord.*

20. Strong, 22.

21. Merriam-Webster. *Unbelief.*

22. Strong, 10.

23. Merriam-Webster. *Fear.*

24. Strong, 59.

25. Ibid., 96

Meet the Author

Tamara Anderson was born in East St. Louis, IL, and raised in Lebanon, IL. She was raised by her grandmother who instilled in her at a very early age to love and fear the Lord. She is the eldest of five, three brothers and a sister, and counts it all joy to have been able to aid in their upbringing. To this day, Tamara, still get phone calls to pray and help them through life lessons. She earned an Associate of Applied Science in Business Management from Southwestern Illinois College. Writing has always been a passion of hers. Mrs. Anderson was just an adolescent when she wrote her first book. She has been married to the world's greatest husband, Paul Anderson, Jr., for almost 13 years. They met in an algebra class in college. At first he was not at all on her radar but God saw fit for her to need his assistance in the class and a wonderful friendship sprang up. As they say, the rest is history and they will celebrate 13 years of marriage in April, 2016.

Tamara is the proud mother of an 18-year-old daughter, Camille Harden. She truly has been her godsend. Being pregnant with her was a wakeup call and Tamara thanks God every day for allowing her to be Camille's mother and for Him blessing her. Camille has graduated high school and her parents are so excited about what her future holds. They know she will be someone great and be used by God in tremendous ways. When Camille was around 2 or 3, Tamara was told of the calling on her life, and the enemy has tried numerous times in the past 18 years to take her but God has said NO every time. They can't wait to see what He has planned for her life; they know it will be grand.

Mrs. Anderson is the delighted grandmother of Landon Jackson. He was born this past January and in his few weeks of life, he has brought so much joy to the household. She just knows that he is going to be a Mighty Man of Valor.

Tamara thanks God for her mother and especially her grandmother, Mother Ina Neal. Her granny, as she is called by everyone, is everything anyone would want their grandmother to be. She is kind, compassionate, caring, strong, and a bible toting prayer warrior. Her love and devotion for the Lord has been such an inspiration to Tamara. While she loves her mom and is so grateful to her, she genuinely thanks Jesus daily that He allowed her granny to raise her because to see her in action categorically changed her life. There is no doubt in

Tamara's mind that she is who she is because of her granny being who she is in God.

Lastly, Tamara would like to thank the Lord for her spiritual father and mother, Bishop Gregory and First Lady Joyce Wells, Sr. They have seen her through some challenging times and she is so grateful to them for their love and support. Being a member of O'Fallon Apostolic Assembly in O'Fallon, IL, has granted her the opportunity to grow in her walk with the Lord through the preached gospel and the occasions of holding several offices. They have permitted Tamara to serve as the former Superintendent of Sunday School, Vice President of Hospitality and Vice President of the Pastor's Aide Committee and currently as the President of the Women's Ministry. Tamara Anderson has been told that her love for souls, positive attitude, gift for administration, and willingness to serve makes her a true asset to the Body of Christ.

Upcoming Publications

Fit For Your Future
(Summer 2016)

With Love
(Fall 2016)

48313085R00098

Made in the USA
San Bernardino, CA
22 April 2017